Understanding German Accounts

Series Editor: Silvano Levy BA, MIL, PhD

Understanding German Accounts

Adelheid Höffgen

Johanna Duncalf-Edelsbacher

PITMAN
PUBLISHING

PITMAN PUBLISHING
128 Long Acre, London WC2E 9AN

A Division of Longman Group Limited

First published 1994

© Longman Group Limited 1994

A CIP catalogue record for this book can be obtained from the British Library.

ISBN 0 273 60309 4

10 9 8 7 6 5 4 3 2 1

Typeset by ROM-Data Corporation Ltd, Falmouth, Cornwall
Printed and bound in Great Britain by Page Bros Ltd

The Publishers' policy is to use paper manufactured from sustainable forests.

Contents

Vorwort

Das Anliegen dieses Buches ist, zweisprachig und in klarer und übersichtlicher Form die Grundprinzipien des deutschen Rechnungswesens anhand von Jahresabschlüssen verschiedenster deutscher Firmen darzustellen und zu erklären.

Der neue Ansatz des Buches besteht darin, daß authentische Jahresabschlüsse zum Ausgangspunkt gemacht wurden. Das heißt, die einzelnen Bestandteile eines Jahresabschlusses – Lagebericht, Bilanz, Gewinn- und Verlustrechnung und Anhang – bestimmen die Gliederung des Buches. Ganz neu ist auch die Untergliederung der Kapitel über Bilanz und Gewinn- und Verlustrechnung, die dem Aufbau einer deutschen Bilanz bzw. Gewinn- und Verlustrechnung entsprechen und gleichzeitig in Wörterbuchform zweisprachig angelegt sind.

Die Kapitel über die einzelnen Bestandteile des Jahresabschlusses werden durch einleitende Erklärungen der Prinzipien und des Inhalts des Jahresabschlusses eines Unternehmens ergänzt. Außerdem finden sich authentische Jahresabschlüsse, Übungen zur Selbstüberprüfung und ein zweisprachiges Glossar am Ende des Buches. Die amerikanische Terminologie wurde ebenfalls miteinbezogen.

Das Buch wendet sich vor allem an Sprachstudenten mit Interesse an bzw. Wahlfach Wirtschaft, die sich aber nicht unbedingt auf Rechnungswesen spezialisieren. Jedoch sind die Informationen und Erklärungen ebenso für Übersetzer, Geschäftsleute und Sekretärinnen von Nutzen.

Preface

The aim of this book is to present and explain the basic principles of German accountancy by means of annual reports published by German companies. This is done in a simple and clear manner and in bilingual form throughout.

Our approach is new in that authentic annual reports form the basis of the book. This means the individual parts of an annual report – directors' report, balance sheet, profit and loss account and notes – dictate the presentation of the book. Moreover, the chapters on the balance sheet and profit and loss account follow the structure of a German balance sheet and profit and loss account and are set out in bilingual dictionary form.

The sections on the individual parts of annual reports also provide introductory explanations of the principles and the content of annual reports. In addition to this, there are actual specimen accounts, exercises for self-study and a bilingual glossary at the end of the book. American terminology has also been included where applicable.

The book is aimed particularly at language students with a business option or interest in business who nevertheless do not specialise in accountancy. However, the information and explanations contained in this book make it extremely useful for translators, business people and secretaries.

Abkürzungen und Symbole
Abbreviations and symbols

Abkürzungen
Abbreviations

Abs.	**Absatz** (section of a law)	
AG	**Aktiengesellschaft** (similar to public limited company (plc) [stock corporation])	
AktG	**Aktiengesetz** (Companies Act for plc [Stock Corporation Law])	
bzw.	**beziehungsweise** (and/or, and . . . respectively)	
d.h.	**das heißt** (that is)	
EStG	**Einkommensteuergesetz** (Income Taxes Act)	
GmbH	**Gesellschaft mit beschränkter Haftung** (similar to private limited company (Ltd Co) [private limited liability company])	
GmbHG	**Gesetz betreffend Gesellschaft mit beschränkter Haftung** (Companies Act for limited company [Private Limited Liability Company Law])	
HGB	**Handelsgesetzbuch** (Commercial Law)	
Mio	**Million** (million)	
Mrd	**Milliarde** (thousand million) [billion]	
PublG	**Publizitätsgesetz** (law covering publication requirements for annual reports)	
z.B.	**zum Beispiel** (for example)	

Symbole
Symbols

*	**englische Standardterminologie**	(standard UK terminology (Companies Act 1985))
(. . .)	**Erklärung**	(explanation)
(= . . .)	**bedeutet**	(equals)
[. . .]	**amerikanischer Begriff**	(US term)
[US]	**amerikanischer Begriff**	(US term)
/	**gleichbedeutend**	(equivalent)
(-)	**Plural**	(plural)
(*pl*)	**Plural**	(plural)
(*sep*)	**trennbares Verb**	(separable verb)
(*refl*)	**reflexives Verb**	(reflexive verb)

1 Einleitung

Introduction

Was ist der Jahresabschluß?

Jedes deutsche Unternehmen hat die gesetzliche Pflicht, Bücher zu führen und am Ende eines bestimmten Zeitraumes einen Jahresabschluß aufzustellen. Je nach Gesellschaftsform (z.B. AG oder GmbH) und Größe des Unternehmens macht der deutsche Gesetzgeber Auflagen über Form, Inhalt und Veröffentlichungspflicht des Jahresabschlusses.

Wir befassen uns in diesem Buch mit Jahresabschlüssen großer Kapitalgesellschaften, die laut Gesetz die umfangreichsten Pflichten über die Aufstellung ihrer Jahresabschlüsse haben. Der Jahresabschluß einer Kapitalgesellschaft besteht aus **Bilanz**, **Gewinn- und Verlustrechnung**, dem **Anhang** und dem **Lagebericht**.

Der Begriff "Bilanz" ist uns aus der Umgangssprache bekannt. Man "zieht Bilanz", d.h. man überblickt einen bestimmten Zeitraum und stellt Vergleiche an zwischen dem, was man "investiert" hat und dem, was dabei herausgekommen ist. Auf ein Unternehmen bezogen bedeutet die **Bilanz** eine Darstellung der finanziellen Bestände des Unternehmens zu einem bestimmten Zeitpunkt, dem Bilanzstichtag. Der betrachtete Zeitraum beträgt normalerweise ein Jahr, das Rechnungsjahr, das aber nicht notwendigerweise mit dem Kalenderjahr übereinstimmt. Die Bilanz eines Rechnungsjahres enthält immer auch die Zahlen des Vorjahres zum Vergleich.

Eine Bilanz zeigt also den finanziellen Zustand des Unternehmens am Bilanzstichtag an und weist aus, ob ein Gewinn oder Verlust gemacht wurde. Sie sagt aber nichts darüber aus, wie dieser Gewinn oder Verlust entstanden ist.

Deshalb wird sie von der **Gewinn- und Verlustrechnung** (Erfolgsrechnung) ergänzt. Diese stellt im Gegensatz zur Bilanz eine Zeitraumrechnung dar, in der die Erträge und Aufwendungen innerhalb der abgerechneten Zeit einander gegenübergestellt werden. Durch sie erfahren wir, wie der Erfolg (Gewinn oder Verlust) zustandegekommen ist.

Die Gliederung der Bilanz und der Gewinn- und Verlustrechnung ist aus Gründen der Übersichtlichkeit und Klarheit sehr knapp gestaltet. Sie folgt bestimmten Konventionen, die im Falle von (externen) Bilanzen großer Firmen, insbesondere Aktiengesellschaften, gesetzlichen Vorschriften unterliegen (HGB und AktG bzw.

GmbHG). (Näheres siehe Kapitel 3 über Bilanzen und Kapitel 4 über Gewinn- und Verlustrechnung.)

Zur Ergänzung und Erläuterung der knappen Bilanz und Gewinn- und Verlustrechnung gibt es noch den Anhang und den Lagebericht. Beide enthalten zusätzliche Informationen, die aus Bilanz und Gewinn- und Verlustrechnung nicht zu ersehen sind.

Der **Anhang** enthält größtenteils zusätzliche Informationen zu den einzelnen Posten der Bilanz und Erfolgsrechnung und untergliedert diese weiter. Außerdem enthält er Angaben über die angewandten Rechnungsgrundsätze und -methoden und ihre Veränderungen gegenüber dem Vorjahr. Die Bilanz und Erfolgsrechnung enthalten im Prinzip immer die gleichen Posten. Der Anhang kann jedoch von Fall zu Fall verschieden aussehen, zumindest können verschiedene Schwerpunkte gesetzt werden, da das deutsche Gesetz eine gewisse Flexibilität erlaubt.

Um ein wirklich umfassendes Bild von der wirtschaftlichen Lage eines Unternehmens zu bekommen, braucht der Interessierte noch ein letztes Papier: den **Lagebericht**. Er wird vom Vorstand (der Geschäftsleitung) erstellt und ist ebenfalls gesetzlicher Bestandteil des Jahresabschlusses. Im Lagebericht findet man wichtige Informationen über die Wirtschaftslage des Unternehmens sowie Entwicklungstendenzen nicht nur der einzelnen Firma, sondern auch der Branche, der Einzel- und Weltkonjunktur. Diese Informationen können aus Bilanz, Erfolgsrechnung sowie Anhang nicht entnommen werden. Die ausführlichen Erklärungen des Lageberichts füllen das Zahlen-Skelett der Bilanz und Erfolgsrechnung mit inhaltlichem Fleisch und Blut. Aus diesem Grund ist der Lagebericht ein äußerst wichtiger Bestandteil in einem Jahresabschluß.

Die Informationen, die der Jahresabschluß enthält, sind für verschiedene Personenkreise von Interesse. Innerhalb des deutschen Jahresabschlusses gilt dies besonders für die Bilanz. Daher gibt es verschiedene Arten von Bilanzen. Man unterscheidet zunächst zwischen internen und externen Bilanzen. Interne Bilanzen dienen der Selbstinformation, sind nicht für Kreise außerhalb der Firma bestimmt und unterliegen deshalb auch nicht gesetzlichen Vorschriften. Externe Bilanzen werden weiter unterteilt in Steuerbilanzen und Handelsbilanzen. Steuerbilanzen sind leicht veränderte Handelsbilanzen, die nur für Finanzbehörden bestimmt sind, also nicht allgemein veröffentlicht werden. Handelsbilanzen hingegen sind für Gesellschafter, Kreditinstitute, die Presse, potentielle Anleger usw. interessant und stehen unter Veröffentlichungspflicht (PublG). Dieses Buch befaßt sich ausschließlich mit diesen externen, publizierten Berichten, also ausschließlich mit publizierten Jahresabschlüssen.

Die folgenden vier Kapitel gliedern den Jahresabschluß auf. Wir beginnen in Kapitel 2 mit dem Lagebericht, ebenso wie jeder Jahresabschluß einer deutschen Firma mit dem Lagebericht beginnt, und geben vor allem typische Beispiele aus authentischen Lageberichten. Dann folgt in Kapitel 3 eine ausführliche Betrachtung der Bilanz, mit Erklärungen zu ihrem Aufbau und einer zweisprachigen Darstellung, die dem tatsächlichen Aufbau einer Bilanz entspricht. Kapitel 4 hat den gleichen Aufbau wie Kapitel 3 und befaßt sich mit der Erfolgsrechnung. Wie bereits erwähnt, besteht der Anhang zum großen Teil aus Ergänzungen zu den einzelnen Posten der Bilanz und Erfolgsrechnung.

Um die zweisprachige Darstellung in Kapitel 3 und 4 so benutzerfreundlich wie möglich zu machen, haben wir diese Ergänzungen in den jeweiligen Rahmen der Bilanz bzw. Erfolgsrechnung eingepaßt. Das heißt, in den zweisprachigen Darstellungen finden sich unter jedem Posten der Bilanz bzw. Erfolgsrechnung die dazugehörigen Termini aus dem Anhang. Kapitel 5 befaßt sich mit dem erläuternden Teil des Anhangs, der z.B. die Abschreibungsmethoden erklärt und jegliche Abweichungen gegenüber dem Vorjahr begründet. Auch hierzu liefern wir authentische Beispiele.

What is the annual report?

Every German business is required by law to keep books and to prepare an annual report at the end of each accounting period. Depending on the legal form of a business (e.g. AG or GmbH) and the size of a firm, German legislation prescribes the form, content and publication obligations in respect of the annual report.

This book deals with annual reports of large German companies which have the most extensive regulations regarding their financial reporting. The annual report of a company consists of **balance sheet**, **profit and loss account**, the **notes thereto** and the **directors' report**.

The term 'balance' suggests two sides which are in equilibrium, i.e. of the same value. Applied to a business the **balance sheet** is the result of a 'stock-taking' of a business's assets and liabilities which have to be in equilibrium. This stock-taking is done on a certain date, the balance sheet date. The period covered is normally one year, the accounting year, which does not necessarily coincide with the calendar year. The balance sheet of one accounting period always contains the figures of the previous year for comparison.

The balance sheet shows the financial position of a business at the balance sheet date and whether a profit or loss has been made. However, it does not give us any information on how the profit or loss has come about.

Therefore it is complemented by the **profit and loss account**. Unlike the balance sheet, this covers a period of time. Income and expenditure that occurred within this period are listed and a result, profit or loss, is calculated. The profit and loss account shows the make-up of a particular profit or loss and also the size of individual income and expenditure items.

In order to achieve clarity and ease of reading, the structure of the balance sheet and the profit and loss account is short and concise. It follows certain conventions which in the case of external accounts of large companies, particularly plcs, are subject to legal requirements (to be found in the HGB and AktG or GmbHG). (For more information see Chapter 3 on balance sheets and Chapter 4 on profit and loss accounts.)

To complement and explain the concise balance sheet and profit and loss account, the annual report also comprises the notes to the financial statements and the directors' report. Both contain additional information which cannot be obtained from the balance sheet or the profit and loss account.

The **notes to the financial statements** concentrate on additional information to the individual entries of balance sheet and profit and loss account and subdivide them further. In addition to this they also give details on accounting policies and accounting methods adopted as well as changes therein since the last balance sheet date. The balance sheet and profit and loss account are consistently made up of the same entries. The notes may vary from year to year, from company to company, at least in that different items may be emphasised as German legislation permits a certain flexibility.

To arrive at a comprehensive picture of the financial situation of a company an interested party needs a final paper: the **directors' report**. As the name suggests it is drawn up by the company directors and is a legally required part of the annual report. In the directors' report we find important information on the economic and financial standing of the company as well as business trends and developments not just of the individual firm but also of the whole sector, the national and world economies. This contextual information cannot be derived from a balance sheet, profit and loss account or notes. The detailed explanations of the directors' report provide the necessary padding for the skeleton of balance sheet and profit and loss account. It is for this reason that the directors' report represents a very important part of the annual report.

The information provided in an annual report is of interest to different groups of people. Within the German annual report this is especially the case with the balance sheet. For this reason we find different types of balance sheets. First, one distinguishes between internal and external balance sheets. Internal ones are prepared in order to keep a business's own management and workforce informed. They are not intended for parties outside the business and are therefore not subject to legal requirements. External balance sheets are further subdivided into so-called 'tax' balance sheets and commercial balance sheets. Tax balance sheets are commercial balance sheets amended for Inland Revenue purposes only and are therefore not generally available. Commercial balance sheets, however, are of interest to shareholders, banks, the press, potential investors, etc. and are required to be published by law (PublG). This book deals exclusively with external accounts and reports, that is exclusively with published annual reports.

The following four chapters are divided according to the four parts of the annual report. Chapter 2 deals with the first item, the directors' report, just as every annual report of a German company starts with the directors' report. It also includes typical examples from real-life directors' reports. Chapter 3 looks at the balance sheet in more detail. It explains its format, content, terminology, etc. and, as its main part, presents a comprehensive bilingual list of balance sheet entries which follows the actual layout of a balance sheet. Chapter 4 deals with the profit and loss account and is structured in the same way as Chapter 3. As mentioned above, a large part of the notes represents those complementing the individual entries of the balance sheet and profit and loss account.

To make the bilingual section of Chapters 3 and 4 as user-friendly as possible, we have added these notes to the respective balance sheet and profit and loss account entries in the bilingual listing. This means under each item from the balance sheet and profit and loss account you also find the appropriate terms from the note thereto. Chapter 5 deals with the notes to the financial statements in detail and explains, for example, the methods of depreciation and any changes since the last balance sheet date. Again we provide examples from existing companies.

2 Der Lagebericht

The directors' report

Was ist der Lagebericht?

In deutschen Jahresabschlüssen ist es üblich, den Lagebericht an den Anfang zu stellen. Er enthält im wesentlichen allgemeine Angaben über die Wirtschaftslage und -entwicklung des Unternehmens und stellt einen integralen Bestandteil des Jahresabschlusses dar.

Im einzelnen sind oft folgende Bereiche im Lagebericht zu finden:

- **die Entwicklung des Geschäftsablaufs im Geschäftsjahr des Jahresabschlusses.** Dazu gehören wichtige Ereignisse wie Erweiterung des Geschäfts, Änderungen in der Produktion, usw.

- **die Lage des Unternehmens im Vergleich zum vergangenen Jahr** bzw. im Kontext von Wirtschaftsindikatoren.

- **Vorgänge von besonderer Bedeutung, die seit Ende des Geschäftsjahres eingetreten sind** und daher sonst nirgends erfaßt sind. Hier sind Ereignisse gemeint, die das gesamte Unternehmen betreffen. Beispiele wären der Verlust eines bedeutenden Vertrags, der Verkauf einer Tochtergesellschaft oder der Tod eines Geschäftsführers.

- **die voraussichtliche Entwicklung des Unternehmens**, z.B. Ausbau des Exportgeschäfts, voraussichtliche Preisentwicklung, usw.

- **die Forschungs- und Entwicklungstätigkeit des Unternehmens.**

Vergleichsmöglichkeiten für diese Bereiche sind gegeben durch Angaben über:

a die Zahlen des Vorjahres, sowie
b die Vorgänge in der Branche als ganzes, in der unser Unternehmen tätig ist, und
c internationale und nationale Trends.

Der Kontext und die Vergleichszahlen steigern die Aussagekraft eines Geschäftsberichts erheblich. Ein Beispiel soll dies verdeutlichen. Der gegenwärtige Gewinnrückgang eines Unternehmens ist vielleicht nicht so bedeutend, wenn man in Betracht zieht, daß es in der Baubranche tätig ist und landesweit eine Rezession auf dem Baumarkt herrscht.

Im deutschen Gesetz ist nicht genau festgelegt, welche Angaben im Lagebericht gemacht werden müssen. Es gibt keine Vorschrift über genaue Zahlenangaben, Tendenzen genügen. Ebenso sind auch freiwillige zusätzliche Angaben möglich. Häufig finden sich im Lagebericht noch Informationen über die Mitarbeiter, ihre Anzahl, Vorsorge der Firma für behinderte Mitarbeiter, freiwillige Sozialleistungen, usw.

Das wichtigste Kriterium eines Lageberichts ist, daß er im Einklang steht mit den Zahlen und Informationen in der Bilanz, der Erfolgsrechnung und im Anhang, das heißt, der Leser darf nicht irregeführt werden. Es ist beispielsweise einem Unternehmen nicht erlaubt, in einem Fünf-Jahresbericht nur die Gewinne der vorangegangenen fünf Jahre und nicht den Verlust des gegenwärtigen Jahres anzuführen. Die diesjährigen Ergebnisse müssen immer miteinbezogen werden, d.h. in diesem Fall die Gewinne der letzten vier Jahre und der Verlust dieses Jahres.

What is the directors' report?

In Germany, the directors' report [corporate management report in the US] is found at the beginning of the annual report. It informs generally on the economic circumstances and developments of a business and is an integral part of the annual report of a company.

The following details are often found in the directors' report:

- **The development of operations in the accounting period of the annual report**. This part contains information on important decisions like expansion of the business or changes in production lines.

- **The state of the business in the context of previous years** (i.e. comparisons) as well as in the context of economic indicators.

- **Post-balance sheet events**. These are events of great significance to the business which took place after the balance sheet date and could therefore not be quantified in the accounts. These events usually affect the whole business. Examples would be the loss of a major contract, the sale of a subsidiary or the death of a director.

- **The expected future development of the business**, e.g. expansion of exports or estimated cost-level changes.

- **The research and development activities of the business.**

Comparisons contained within a directors' report may include:

a last year's figures;
b the broader context of the specific business sector's performance; and
c national and worldwide trends.

Contextual details and comparative figures increase the information value of financial statements considerably. One example may illustrate this. A business's current reduction in profits may be less significant if the sector is 'construction' and the recession in the housing market is nationwide.

The content of a German directors' report is not regulated by statute. It is permissible to give indications of trends, instead of precise figures. One may also find supplementary information which is provided voluntarily. Further details on employees, such as number of employees, provisions for disabled employees, voluntary additional payments like private health care, are also often found in directors' reports.

The most important criterion of a directors' report is that it is consistent with the figures and information in the balance sheet, profit and loss account and notes, i.e. it does not mislead the reader. For example, a five-year report cannot exclude the loss of the current year and only include the previous five years' profits. The result of the current accounting period must always be incorporated. That means, in this case, the five-year report must comprise the profits of the previous four years and the loss of the current year.

Beispiele
Examples

The following examples from real-life directors' reports were selected because of their significance and frequency of use. They are divided into three groups.

Informationen zur allgemeinen Wirtschaftslage

Information on the economic environment

1. die Konjunkturschwäche in den meisten Industrieländern
2. Der Welthandel wuchs real nur um drei Prozent nach doppelt so hohen Zuwachsraten Ende der achtziger Jahre.
3. In Nordamerika nahmen die Umsätze um elf Prozent zu.
4. Die Experten rechnen nicht damit, daß sich die Wirtschaftslage in den nächsten Monaten merklich verbessern wird.
5. Die wirtschaftliche Aufwärtsentwicklung setzte sich weiter fort.
6. Unsere Auslandsmärkte wurden von der anhaltenden Konjunkturschwäche beeinflußt.
7. Der Kampf um Marktanteile verstärkte sich.
8. Die Veränderungen der Wechselkurse schlagen stark zu Buche.
9. In einigen europäischen Ländern bessert sich die Stimmung über die weitere wirtschaftliche Entwicklung.
10. Im Tourismus wird weiterhin von einem guten Geschäftsverlauf ausgegangen.

Informationen zum Unternehmen

Information on the business

1. Das Geschäftsjahr 1993 schließt erstmals seit 1973 mit einem Bilanzverlust.
2. Das wirtschaftliche Eigenkapital – Nennkapital, Rücklagen und 50 Prozent des Sonderpostens mit Rücklageanteil – nahm um 580 Millionen DM ab.
3. Die Eigenkapitalquote ist auf 25,7 Prozent gesunken.
4. Der Weltumsatz stieg um 4%.
5. Die Investitionen in Sachanlagen haben wir gesteigert.
6. Der Jahresüberschuß nahm um 6% auf 52 Mio DM zu.
7. In den neuen Bundesländern sind wir mit eigenständigen Gesellschaften tätig.
8. Die unterschiedlichen Strukturen und Tendenzen in Ost- und Westdeutschland erfordern derzeit noch eine getrennte Bewertung.
9. Der Anstieg des privaten Verbrauchs betrug real 2,5%.
10. Der reale Umsatzzuwachs belief sich auf 5,6%.
11. eine Reihe kleinerer Akquisitionen
12. Es ergaben sich Umsatzeinbußen in Höhe von 2,8 Mrd DM. Dies entspricht 6% des Konzernumsatzes.
13. Steigerung des Gewinns
14. In beiden Geschäftsbereichen mußten wir Verluste hinnehmen.
15. Wir haben unseren Forschungsaufwand weltweit auf 2,7 Mrd DM erhöht.
16. Wir konnten Aufträge in Höhe von 82,2 Mrd DM hereinholen. Das bedeutet eine Steigerung um 21%.
17. Wir weiteten die Sachanlageinvestitionen kräftig aus.
18. gestiegene Ausgaben für Forschung und Entwicklung
19. Unser Gewinn nach Steuern erhöhte sich.
20. Das Anlagevermögen stieg um 0,8 Mrd DM, das Umlaufvermögen um 4,2 Mrd DM.
21. Der anhaltende Kostendruck erfordert weitere Rationalisierungsmaßnahmen.
22. Wir finanzierten die Forschungs- und Entwicklungsaufwendungen fast vollständig aus eigenen Erträgen.

Informationen über Mitarbeiter

Information on employees

1. Die Personalaufwendungen bilden nach wie vor den größten Kostenblock.
2. Die Zahl unserer Mitarbeiter nahm um 2% zu.

3. Wir haben in die Förderung der Qualifikation des Personals erheblich investiert.
4. die Betriebskrankenkasse der Firma
5. betriebliche Versorgungsleistungen
6. Die sozialen Abgaben stiegen wegen Erhöhung des Beitragssatzes in der Arbeitslosenversicherung.
7. Die Zahl der Beschäftigten stieg auf 172 890 Mitarbeiter.
8. Die Zahl der Mitarbeiter ist sprunghaft gestiegen.
9. Der Rückgang der Mitarbeiterzahl betrifft vor allem Standorte außerhalb Deutschlands.
10. Für die Aus- und Weiterbildung wendeten wir im Berichtsjahr 690 Mio DM auf.

3 Die Bilanz

The balance sheet

Was ist die Bilanz?

Wie bereits in der Einleitung erwähnt, stellt die Bilanz die Beständerechnung eines Unternehmens am Ende eines Jahres dar. Diese Bestandsaufnahme geschieht in Form einer Gegenüberstellung, das heißt, eine deutsche Bilanz hat zwei Seiten. Die beiden Seiten werden **Aktiva** (links) und **Passiva** (rechts) genannt. Da der Begriff "Bilanz" "Gleichgewicht" bedeutet, müssen die Aktiva den Passiva zahlenmäßig genau entsprechen.

Um die Bilanz zu erklären, fängt man am besten mit den Passiva an. Diese stellen die Mittelherkunft oder Finanzierung eines Unternehmens dar, also das Kapital, welches in die Firma einfließt. Es wird dazu verwendet, die Firma aufzubauen und sie in Betrieb zu halten. Dieses Kapital kommt aus verschiedenen Quellen, die in zwei große Gruppen eingeteilt werden: **Eigenkapital** und **Fremdkapital.**

Eigenkapital kommt, wie der Name sagt, aus eigenen Quellen, also Aktien (AG) bzw. Geschäftsanteile (GmbH) und Rücklagen. Rücklagen sind vorwiegend Gewinne, die aus eigener Geschäftätigkeit erwirtschaftet und im Unternehmen zurückbehalten wurden.

Das **Fremdkapital** beinhaltet auf der einen Seite alle Kredite, die das Unternehmen von außen bekommt, also z.B. Bankdarlehen und Lieferantenkredite. Diese werden als Verbindlichkeiten bezeichnet und können langfristig oder kurzfristig sein. Auf der anderen Seite finden sich im Fremdkapital auch die Rückstellungen. Diese Rückstellungen werden für wahrscheinlich anfallende Aufwände gebildet, z.B. ausstehende Rechnungen und drohende Verluste. (Nähere Erklärungen gibt der Abschnitt "Passiva" in diesem Kapitel.)

Die Aktivseite der Bilanz zeigt das Vermögen, also was das Unternehmen "aktiv" mit seinem Kapital macht. Diese Seite umfaßt alle Wirtschaftsgüter und Geldmittel, die im Betrieb eingesetzt werden. Dazu gehören zum Beispiel Gebäude und Maschinen, aber auch Bankguthaben und Bargeld. Ebenso gehören zu den Aktiva sämtliche Forderungen des Unternehmens. Das sind Schulden, die andere bei unserem Unternehmen haben. Ihnen stehen auf der Passivseite die Verbindlichkeiten der Firma gegenüber. Ebenso wie jene können die Forderungen kurz- oder langfristig sein.

Eine deutsche Bilanz wird als direkte Gegenüberstellung angeordnet, also Aktiva links, Passiva rechts, wie folgt:

Aktiva	Passiva
Vermögen	Eigenkapital Fremdkapital

Die Aktiva

Die linke Seite einer Bilanz umfaßt drei Gruppen:

- Anlagevermögen
- Umlaufvermögen
- Rechnungsabgrenzungsposten

ANLAGEVERMÖGEN

Wie aus dem Begriff "Anlage" zu ersehen ist, handelt es sich um Güter, die langfristig angelegt sind. Dazu gehören Grundstücke, Gebäude, Maschinen, usw.
Das Anlagevermögen wird in der Bilanz wiederum in drei Teile gegliedert.

1. IMMATERIELLE VERMÖGENSGEGENSTÄNDE

Sie beinhalten vor allem langfristig erworbene Rechte, z.B. Patente, Konzessionen, Lizenzen. Dazu gehört auch der Firmenwert oder Geschäftswert. Er umfaßt solche "immateriellen" Werte wie guter Ruf der Firma, der wertvolle Kundenstamm, oder der Wert eines Markenartikels. Dieser Firmenwert ist besonders schwer zu erfassen, und darf nur in der Bilanz erscheinen, wenn beim Kauf des Unternehmens für ihn etwas bezahlt wurde.

2. SACHANLAGEN (MATERIELLE VERMÖGENSGEGENSTÄNDE)

Hierzu gehören alle konkreten, faßbaren Güter wie Grundstücke, Gebäude, Maschinen, Werkzeuge, Fahrzeuge. Die meisten dieser Gegenstände verlieren allmählich ihren Wert und unterliegen daher einer Wertminderung oder Abschreibung. (Erklärung des Begriffs Abschreibung siehe Kapitel 5 über Anhang.)

3. FINANZANLAGEN

Hierzu gehören alle Arten von Wertpapieren, vor allem Beteiligungen (Investitionen) an anderen Firmen, die im Besitz/Teilbesitz des Unternehmens sind. Dazu kommen langfristige Darlehensforderungen.

UMLAUFVERMÖGEN

Auch hier läßt der Begriff erkennen, daß es sich dabei um kurzfristige Vermögensgegenstände handelt. Kurzfristig bedeutet gewöhnlich maximal 12 Monate, also ein Geschäftsjahr. Das heißt, daß am Ende des nächsten Geschäftsjahres voraussichtlich diese Vorräte abgesetzt, diese Forderungen eingegangen und diese Wertpapiere verkauft sein werden.

Das Umlaufvermögen wird in vier Gruppen eingeteilt.

1. VORRÄTE

Dazu gehören Rohstoffe (Eisen, Baumwolle, usw.), Hilfs- und Betriebsstoffe (Farben, Leim, Werkzeuge, usw.), unfertige und fertige Erzeugnisse.

2. FORDERUNGEN UND SONSTIGE VERMÖGENSGEGENSTÄNDE

Diese sind hauptsächlich unbezahlte Kundenrechnungen, aber auch z.B. Forderungen an verbundene Unternehmen.

3. WERTPAPIERE

Die Wertpapiere der Umlaufvermögens werden im Gegensatz zu Finanzanlagen nur kurzfristig gehalten, d.h. das Unternehmen beabsichtigt, sie innerhalb von 12 Monaten zu verkaufen.

4. FLÜSSIGE MITTEL (ZAHLUNGSMITTEL)

Sie beinhalten im wesentlichen Bankguthaben, Postgiroguthaben und Kassenbestände.

RECHNUNGSABGRENZUNGSPOSTEN

Als letzte Position auf der Aktivseite der Bilanz finden sich die sogenannten Rechnungsabgrenzungsposten. Sie kommen dadurch zustande, daß das Geschäftsjahr zwar zu einem bestimmten Zeitpunkt, dem Bilanzstichtag, endet, aber nicht alle Geschäfte genau in diesen Zeitraum passen. Ein Beispiel dafür sind Löhne oder Mieten, die vor dem Bilanzstichtag bezahlt worden sind, aber erst einen Zeitraum nach dem Bilanzstichtag betreffen. Sie gehören also noch zum Vermögen der Firma. Sie müssen in der Bilanz "aktivisch" abgegrenzt werden, um deutlich zu machen, daß sie in den nächsten Zeitraum gehören.

Die Struktur innerhalb jeder Gruppe von Vermögensgegenständen ist genauso angelegt wie auf der gesamten Vermögens- sowie Kapitalseite. Das bedeutet, langfristige Vermögensgegenstände erscheinen zuerst, danach folgen in logischer Abfolge immer kurzfristigere Gegenstände.

Einige Beispiele verdeutlichen dies.

- Grundstücke und Gebäude werden normalerweise nicht so oft ersetzt wie technische Anlagen und Maschinen und werden daher als langfristiger angesehen.
- Vorräte werden durch Verkauf zu Forderungen und dann durch Bezahlung zu Bargeld. Dieser Prozeß wird durch ihre Position verdeutlicht:
    1. Vorräte
    2. Forderungen
    3. Bargeld
- Wertpapiere sind langfristiger festgelegt als einfache Bankguthaben, daher erscheinen sie in der Bilanz zuerst.

Eine Ausnahme in dieser Struktur bilden die Rechnungsabgrenzungsposten, die aus Gründen der Klarheit getrennt und am Ende der Aktivseite stehen, obwohl sie im allgemeinen kurzfristig sind.

Dieselbe Struktur findet sich auf der Passivseite einer Bilanz.

Die Passiva

Die rechte Seite einer Bilanz umfaßt vier Gruppen:

- Eigenkapital
- *Sonderposten mit Rücklageanteil*
- Rückstellungen
- Verbindlichkeiten ⎫
- Rechnungsabgrenzungsposten ⎬ Fremdkapital

Rückstellungen, Verbindlichkeiten und Rechnungsabgrenzungsposten werden als "Fremdkapital" zusammengefaßt, um sie vom Eigenkapital abzugrenzen. Diese Terminologie bezieht sich auf die Art der **Finanzierung eines Unternehmens**, also die Quellen des Kapitals.

Eigenkapital ist die Finanzierung des Unternehmens durch Aktionäre bzw. Anteilseigner, die dem Unternehmen langfristig Mittel zur Verfügung stellen. Die Aktionäre erwerben durch den Kauf von Aktien einen Anteil an dem Unternehmen. Sie erhalten dafür eine Gewinnbeteiligung, die Dividende. Allerdings hat ein Unternehmen eine gewisse Flexibilität, weil die Dividende in schwierigen Zeiten gekürzt oder gestrichen werden können.

Fremdkapital stellt Finanzierung von außen dar, hauptsächlich durch langfristige und kurzfristige Darlehen. Die Bedingungen der Fremdfinanzierung sind weit weniger flexibel als die der Eigenfinanzierung, denn der Darlehensgeber verlangt die Tilgung seines Darlehens und die Zinszahlungen, egal ob das

Unternehmen einen Gewinn gemacht hat oder nicht. In schwierigen Zeiten kann es passieren, daß ein Unternehmen seinen Darlehensverpflichtungen nicht nachkommen kann. Das kann so weit führen, daß ein Unternehmen vom Darlehensgeber in den Konkurs gezwungen wird, weil nicht genügend flüssige Mittel vorhanden sind.

Aus diesem Grund ist es vorteilhafter, so viel wie möglich Finanzierung über die Aktionäre zu bekommen, also Eigenkapital. Andererseits hat Fremdkapital den Vorteil, daß die Kapitalgeber (zumeist Banken) im allgemeinen weniger Einfluß auf die Geschäftsentscheidungen haben als die Anteilseigner.

EIGENKAPITAL

1. GEZEICHNETES KAPITAL

Diese enthält alle Arten von Stammaktien und Vorzugsaktien.

2. KAPITALRÜCKLAGE

Diese Rücklage steht normalerweise nicht zur Gewinnausschüttung zur Verfügung. Sie enthält unter anderem Überschüsse, die sich ergeben, wenn Aktien an der Börse über dem Nominalwert verkauft werden.

3. GEWINNRÜCKLAGEN

Diese stehen potentiell zur Gewinnausschüttung zur Verfügung. Es gibt vier Arten von Gewinnrücklagen:

a   gesetzliche Rücklagen, die vom deutschen Gesetzgeber vorgeschrieben sind (im AktG).
b   Rücklagen für eigene Anteile, die dann gebildet werden, wenn das Unternehmen, das eine juristische Person ist, eigene Aktien kaufen will.
c   satzungsmäßige Rücklagen, die von der Satzung des Unternehmens verlangt werden.
d   sonstige Gewinnrücklagen.

4. GEWINNVORTRAG/VERLUSTVORTRAG

Dieser Posten beinhaltet die Gewinne oder Verluste aller vergangenen Jahre.

5. JAHRESÜBERSCHUß/JAHRESFEHLBETRAG

Dieser Posten ist das Endresultat (Saldo) der Gewinn- und Verlustrechnung und wird direkt in die Bilanz übertragen. Er kann durch den Posten **Bilanzgewinn oder -verlust** ersetzt werden. Der Bilanzgewinn/-verlust ist ein leicht veränderter

Jahresüberschuß oder -fehlbetrag. In konsolidierten Jahresabschlüssen findet man hier den Posten **Konzernbilanzgewinn/-verlust** oder Konzerngewinn/-verlust, der dieselbe Bedeutung hat und dem normalerweise der Posten **Anteile im Fremdbesitz** folgt.

SONDERPOSTEN MIT RÜCKLAGEANTEIL

Dieser Posten besteht teils aus Eigenkapital und teils aus Fremdkapital, daher die Bezeichnung 'mit Rücklageanteil'. Er wird zwischen Eigenkapital und Fremdkapital eingefügt und aus diesem Grund 'Sonderposten' genannt.

Man findet einerseits Wertberichtigungen und andererseits steuerfreie Rücklagen unter diesem Posten. Wertberichtigungen sind zusätzliche Abschreibungen oder sogenannte steuerliche Sonderabschreibungen, die das deutsche Steuergesetz erlaubt, und die hier oder auf der Aktivseite erfaßt werden können. Steuerfreie Rücklagen werden gebildet, um Teile des Gewinns vorübergehend der Ertragsbesteuerung zu entziehen. Das bedeutet, daß unbesteuerte Gewinne in diese Rücklagen transferiert werden.

RÜCKSTELLUNGEN

Diese sind langfristige und kurzfristige Verbindlichkeiten in bezug auf Pensionszahlungen und ähnliche Verpflichtungen, sowie in bezug auf Steuern und andere zukünftige Verbindlichkeiten.

VERBINDLICHKEITEN

Es gibt verschiedene Arten von Verbindlichkeiten, von denen einige eine Laufzeit von weniger als einem Jahr haben (auf das Geschäftsjahr bezogen) und andere, die eine Laufzeit von mehr als einem Jahr haben.

Beispiele für Verbindlichkeiten sind: Bankdarlehen und Überziehungskredite, Lieferantenkredite, Verbindlichkeiten gegenüber Konzernmitgliedern, Steuern, die an das Finanzamt zu zahlen sind.

RECHNUNGSABGRENZUNGSPOSTEN

Das sind größtenteils Zahlungen, die fällig sind, aber zum Zeitpunkt der Bilanzaufstellung noch nicht geleistet waren. Sie sind alle sehr kurzfristiger Natur. Sie sind im Prinzip das genaue Spiegelbild der Rechnungsabgrenzungsposten auf der Aktivseite.

What is the balance sheet?

As already mentioned in the introduction, the balance sheet represents a business's assets, capital and liabilities at the end of a financial year. This 'stock-taking' is presented in the form of a comparison, that is the German balance sheet has two sides. These two sides are called 'Aktiva', meaning **assets**, on the left-hand side and 'Passiva', meaning **capital and liabilities**, on the right-hand side. (*Note*: In the United Kingdom the layout of a balance sheet is quite different from that of a German one!)

The term balance sheet refers to the balance or equilibrium that needs to exist between the two sides, assets and capital and liabilities. Both sides always have the same total in Deutsch Mark.

To explain the balance sheet it is best to begin with capital and liabilities (always found on the right-hand side of a German balance sheet). They represent the sources of funds or financing of a business, that is, all the monies flowing into the business to set it up and to keep it operational. These funds come from different sources which can be divided into two groups: 'own funds' or capital and 'outside funds' or liabilities. (*Note*: the German term 'Kapital' in this context is not exactly equivalent to the English term 'capital' – see glossary.)

Own funds, as the name suggests, come from own sources, i.e. shares and reserves. Reserves are largely profits which were acquired through a business's own activities and retained within the business.

Outside funds comprise on the one hand all credit arrangements with parties outside the business, e.g. bank loans and trade creditors. These creditors can be long-term or short-term. On the other hand, provisions for liabilities and charges are also part of the outside funds. These provisions are created for various probable future costs, e.g. accruals (outstanding payments) and pending losses. (See also the section 'Capital and liabilities' later in this chapter.)

The asset side of a balance sheet shows how a business has 'actively' used its funds. Therefore this side comprises all business assets and monies which are employed in operations. It includes, for example, buildings and machines, but also bank deposits and cash. Debtors of a business are also counted as assets. They represent monies owed by others to our business. Debtors (on the assets side) can be compared with creditors (on the capital and liabilities side). In the same way as creditors, debtors can be short-term or long-term.

As noted above, a German balance sheet is presented as a direct comparison, that is, assets on the left, and capital and liabilities on the right (as illustrated below).

Assets	Capital and liabilities
Business assets	Capital (own funds) Liabilities (outside funds)

Assets

The left-hand side of a balance sheet comprises three groups:

● Fixed assets
● Current assets
● Prepayments and accrued income

FIXED ASSETS*

The term 'fixed' indicates that these are assets acquired for long-term use, i.e. land, buildings, machinery, etc.

There are three types of fixed assets.

1. INTANGIBLE (FIXED) ASSETS

These are primarily acquired rights for the long-term future, i.e. patents, concessions, licences. Goodwill is also an intangible fixed asset. When acquiring a business the purchaser may be asked to pay more than the actual value of its assets (consisting of plant, stock, etc.) because of the business's reputation, its stock of customers, or its brand name. Goodwill is particularly difficult to quantify and may only be stated in the balance sheet if the company has paid for it when acquiring the business.

2. TANGIBLE (FIXED) ASSETS

These are long-term tangible or touchable assets like land, buildings, machines, tools, or motor vehicles. Most of these assets lose some of their value over the years, and are therefore subject to depreciation (for an explanation of the term 'depreciation', see Chapter 5, 'Notes to the Financial Statements').

3. INVESTMENTS* [FINANCIAL ASSETS]

These are all types of securities, mainly shares owned by our business in other undertakings and long-term loans (to other parties).

CURRENT ASSETS*

The term 'current' implies that these are assets held for the short-term, to be precise for 12 months or less. This means that by the end of the following year one expects this balance sheet stock to be sold, these balance sheet debts to be collected and these balance sheet investments to be disposed of.

There are four types of current assets.

1. STOCKS* [INVENTORIES]

Stocks comprise raw materials (iron, cloth, etc.), consumables (paint, glue, small tools, etc.), work-in-progress (i.e. semi-finished and/or unfinished goods) and finished goods.

2. DEBTORS [RECEIVABLES] AND OTHER CURRENT ASSETS

These are largely trade debtors, but also amounts owed by, for example, a subsidiary.

3. INVESTMENTS* [SECURITIES]

This is the equivalent of the fixed asset section on investments, with the crucial difference that the company intends to dispose of these investments within 12 months.

4. CASH AT BANK AND IN HAND*

It is precisely what it says, money in business bank accounts and cash in the till or petty cash.

PREPAYMENTS AND ACCRUED INCOME*

The last balance sheet heading on the asset side is Prepayments and accrued income. Prepayments arise because not all business transactions end with the end of the accounting period, i.e. the balance sheet date. An example is salaries or rent paid before the balance sheet date but covering a time period extending beyond the current financial year. At the balance sheet date some (or all) of the amounts paid are prepaid and therefore strictly still an asset. In order to clarify that these amounts belong in the following accounting period they have to be stated as prepayments. Accrued income is income due for the current period but not received by the balance sheet date.

The structure within each group of assets is set up in the same way as the whole section of assets and of capital and liabilities. This means long-term assets are stated first and are then followed in logical sequence by more and more short-term assets.

Some examples may illustrate this.

- Land and buildings are not normally replaced as often as plant and machinery and are therefore considered more long-term.
- Stocks when sold become debtors and these when paid become cash. This process is reflected in their respective positions:
  1. Stocks
  2. Debtors
  3. Cash
- Current asset investments are held on a more long-term basis than cash and therefore appear first in the balance sheet.

An exception to this structure is the item 'Prepayments and accrued income' which for reasons of clarity is always stated separately and at the end of the assets section although it is generally of a short-term nature.

The same structure is found on the capital and liabilities side of a balance sheet.

Capital and liabilities

The right-hand side of a balance sheet comprises four groups:

- Capital and reserves
- *Special tax-allowable reserve*
- Provisions ⎫
- Creditors ⎬ Liabilities
- Accruals and deferred income ⎭

Provisions, Creditors and Accruals and deferred income are called outside funds or liabilities in order to distinguish them from own funds or capital. These two terms refer to the type of **financing**, i.e. the sources of funds of a business.

Own funds represent financing through shareholders who provide cash on a long-term basis. These shareholders acquire a stake or interest in the business by buying shares. As a reward they receive a part of the profits, the dividends.

However, the directors of a company have a certain flexibility in that at difficult times dividends can be reduced or not paid at all.

Outside funds represent financing from outside the business, mainly long-term and short-term loans. The conditions of outside financing are far less flexible than those of own financing because the loan provider demands repayment of the loan plus interest regardless of whether the company makes a profit or not. Therefore, at difficult times, a business may not be able to meet its loan obligations. It can even result in the loan provider forcing the business into liquidation because of insufficient cash.

For this reason, it is advantageous to obtain as much finance as possible from shareholders. On the other hand, loan providers (mostly banks in Germany) have generally much less influence than shareholders on business decisions.

CAPITAL AND RESERVES* [EQUITY]

1. NOMINAL CAPITAL [SUBSCRIBED CAPITAL]

This includes all types of ordinary shares as well as preference shares.

2. CAPITAL RESERVE

This reserve is not usually distributable to shareholders. An example would be share premiums, which arise when shares are sold above par value.

3. REVENUE RESERVES

These are potentially distributable as dividends. There are four types of revenue reserves:
a   legal reserves which are required by law (AktG).
b   reserve for own shares which is created if the company itself as a legal entity intends to buy its own shares.
c   reserves as per articles of association which are required by a company's own rules.
d   other revenue reserves.

4. RETAINED PROFITS/ACCUMULATED LOSSES BROUGHT FORWARD (PROFIT AND LOSS ACCOUNT BROUGHT FORWARD)

This item represents all previous years' profits and/or losses.

5. PROFIT OR LOSS FOR THE YEAR

This is the net profit or net loss directly transferred from the profit and loss account into the balance sheet. Sometimes the balance sheet heading **Balance sheet profit** or **Balance sheet loss** is found instead. It represents a slightly adjusted profit or loss figure for the year. In consolidated accounts it is called **Group profit** or **Group loss**, which is usually followed by **Minority interests**.

SPECIAL TAX-ALLOWABLE RESERVE

This special reserve is a mixture of capital and liabilities, hence its special position between capital and liabilities.

It comprises, on the one hand, adjustments to assets, and, on the other, tax-free reserves. Adjustments to assets constitute special additional depreciation permitted by German tax law which may be included here instead of on the assets side. Tax-free reserves are created in order to hold back temporarily some of the profits from taxation; it is a temporary tax haven. This means that it is untaxed profits that are transferred into these tax-free reserves.

PROVISIONS FOR LIABILITIES AND CHARGES

These represent long-term and short-term liabilities in respect of pensions and similar obligations as well as of taxation and other future liabilities. (In the United Kingdom provisions for liabilities and charges consist of long-term items only.)

CREDITORS [ACCOUNTS PAYABLE/LIABILITIES]

There are many types of creditors some of which are amounts falling due within one year (of the balance sheet date), others amounts falling due after more than one year.

Examples of creditors are: bank loans and overdrafts, trade creditors (suppliers), amounts owed to group undertakings, tax payable to the Inland Revenue.

ACCRUALS AND DEFERRED INCOME*

Accruals are payments due but not yet made at the balance sheet date. Deferred income is income received but relating to future accounting periods. All items included in this section are very short-term liabilities. In principle they are the mirror image of 'Prepayments and accrued income' on the assets side.

Die Bilanzposten: Deutsch—Englisch

Balance sheet entries: German—English

This chapter represents a **bilingual presentation of a balance sheet** following the structure of real-life German balance sheets. The entries under each heading are listed in alphabetical order to make reference easier.

As a balance sheet is generally read in conjunction with the notes to the financial statements we have included terminology from these notes under the respective balance sheet headings.

Aktiva

Assets

ANLAGEVERMÖGEN	FIXED ASSETS*

IMMATERIELLE VERMÖGENSGEGENSTÄNDE	INTANGIBLE ASSETS*

Abgänge	disposals
Abschreibungen	amortisation charges
Anlagenspiegel	fixed asset schedule
Anschaffungs- und Herstellungskosten	acquisition costs and manufacturing costs
Buchwerte	net book values
Firmenwert	goodwill*
geleistete Anzahlungen	payments on account* [prepaid expenses]
Geschäftswert	goodwill*

33

gewerbliche Schutzrechte und ähnliche Rechte	patents, licences, trademarks and similar rights
Konzessionen	concessions
Konzessionen, gewerbliche Schutzrechte und ähnliche Rechte und Werte	concessions, patents, licences, trade marks and similar rights and assets*
kumulierte Abschreibungen	accumulated amortisation
Umbuchungen	transfers
Zugänge	additions

SACHANLAGEN	TANGIBLE ASSETS*
Abgänge	disposals
Abschreibungen	depreciation charges
andere Anlagen	other plant
Anlagenspiegel	fixed asset schedule
Anschaffungs- und Herstellungskosten	acquisition costs and manufacturing costs
Bauten auf fremden Grundstücken	buildings on third-party land
Betriebs- und Geschäftsausstattung	fixtures and fittings of plant and office
Buchwerte	net book values
geleistete Anzahlungen und Anlagen im Bau	payments on account and assets in course of construction*
Grundstücke	land
grundstücksgleiche Rechte und Bauten	rights equivalent to real property / leasehold rights
kumulierte Abschreibungen	accumulated depreciation
technische Anlagen und Maschinen	plant and machinery* (= factory equipment)
Umbuchungen	transfers
vermietete Erzeugnisse	manufactured assets rented out, manufactured equipment leased (to customers)
Zugänge	additions

FINANZANLAGEN	INVESTMENTS* [FINANCIAL ASSETS] (= long-term investments)
Abgänge	disposals
Abschreibungen	amounts written off investments
Anlagenspiegel	fixed asset schedule
Anschaffungskosten	purchase prices/acquisition costs
Anteile an assoziierten Unternehmen	shares in associated undertakings
Anteile an verbundenen Unternehmen	shares in group undertakings* [shares in affiliated enterprises]
Ausleihungen an Unternehmen, mit denen ein Beteiligungsverhältnis besteht	loans to undertakings in which the company has a participating interest* [loans to enterprises in which participations are held]
Ausleihungen an verbundene Unternehmen	loans to group undertakings* [loans to affiliated enterprises]
Beteiligungen	participating interests* [participations] (This can include associated undertakings.)
Buchwerte	net book values
Miet- und Pachtvorauszahlungen	rent and property lease prepayments (= long-term prepayments)
sonstige Ausleihungen	other loans*
sonstige Finanzanlagen	other investments* (= long-term investments)
Umbuchungen	transfers
Vorfinanzierung von Mietobjekten	advance financing of property rent (= long-term prepayment)
Wertpapiere des Anlagevermögens	long-term investments
Zugänge	additions

UMLAUFVERMÖGEN — CURRENT ASSETS*

VORRÄTE	STOCKS* [INVENTORIES]
Erzeugnisse und Waren	finished goods and goods for resale* [finished goods and merchandise]
fertige Erzeugnisse und Waren	finished goods and goods for resale* [finished goods and merchandise]

geleistete Anzahlungen	payments on account* [prepaid expenses] (= advances to suppliers for stocks ordered but not yet received)
halbfertige Erzeugnisse	work-in-progress* [work-in-process] (= semi-finished goods)
nicht abgerechnete Leistungen	services provided but not invoiced
Roh-, Hilfs- und Betriebsstoffe	raw materials and consumables* [raw materials and supplies]
unfertige Erzeugnisse	work-in-progress* [work-in-process] (= unfinished goods)
unfertige Leistungen	work-in-progress* [work-in-process] (= uncompleted services)
unverrechnete Lieferungen und Leistungen	goods and services (accounts) not balanced off
Vorräte insgesamt	stocks [inventories] (in total)
FORDERUNGEN UND SONSTIGE VERMÖGENSGEGENSTÄNDE	DEBTORS AND OTHER CURRENT ASSETS [RECEIVABLES AND OTHER CURRENT ASSETS]
andere Forderungen und sonstige Vermögensgegenstände	other debtors [receivables] and other current assets
Forderungen aus dem Versicherungsgeschäft	debtors [receivables] from the insurance business
Forderungen aus Lieferungen und Leistungen	debtors* (= amounts owed for goods delivered and services rendered)
• **an Kunden**	• trade debtors* [trade receivables]
• **an verbundene Unternehmen**	• amounts owed by group undertakings* [receivables from affiliated enterprises]
• **an Unternehmen, mit denen ein Beteiligungsverhältnis besteht**	• amounts owed by undertakings in which the company has a participating interest* [receivables from enterprises in which participations are held]
Forderungen gegen Unternehmen, mit denen ein Beteiligungsverhältnis besteht	amounts owed by undertakings in which the company has a participating interest* [receivables from enterprises in which participations are held]
Forderungen gegen verbundene Unternehmen	amounts owed by group undertakings* [receivables from affiliated enterprises]

Forderungen und sonstige Vermögensgegenstände mit einer Restlaufzeit von mehr als einem Jahr	debtors [receivables] and other current assets: amounts due after more than one year
sonstige Vermögensgegenstände	other current assets
WERTPAPIERE	INVESTMENTS* [SHORT-TERM INVESTMENTS/SECURITIES]
Aktien	shares [stocks]
Anteile an verbundenen Unternehmen	shares in group undertakings* [shares in affiliated enterprises]
eigene Aktien	own shares (in AG)*
eigene Anteile	own shares (in GmbH)*
festverzinsliche Wertpapiere	fixed-interest bearing investments (= short-term investments)
sonstige Wertpapiere	other investments* (= short-term investments)
Stammaktien	ordinary shares [common stock/common equity]
Vorzugsaktien	preference shares [preferred stock]
SCHECKS, KASSENBESTAND, BUNDESBANK- UND POSTGIROGUTHABEN, GUTHABEN BEI KREDITINSTITUTEN	CASH AT BANK AND IN HAND* (cheques, cash in hand, central bank and postal giro balances, bank balances)
FLÜSSIGE MITTEL	CASH AT BANK AND IN HAND* (= liquid funds)
Bundesbankguthaben	Bundesbank deposits
Postgiroguthaben	postal giro deposits
RECHNUNGSABGRENZUNGSPOSTEN	PREPAYMENTS AND ACCRUED INCOME*
Disagio	discounts on interest-bearing investments (= difference between the amount received as loan, e.g. 900DM, and the amount to be repaid at repayment date, e.g. 1000DM)
Rechnungsabgrenzungsposten	prepayments and accrued income*
Steuerabgrenzungsposten	prepaid tax (= prepayment) or tax refund not yet received (=accrued income)

Passiva

Capital and liabilities [Liabilities and shareholders' equity]

EIGENKAPITAL	CAPITAL AND RESERVES* [SHAREHOLDERS' EQUITY/ EQUITY] (= shareholders' fund)
GEZEICHNETES KAPITAL	NOMINAL CAPITAL [SUBSCRIBED CAPITAL]
bedingtes Kapital	conditional (authorised unissued) capital (= additional share capital authorised for future issue conditional on conversion rights or share options being exercised)
genehmigtes Kapital	authorised (unissued) capital (= additional share capital authorised for future issue)
Grundkapital	share capital (in AG)
Inhaberaktien	bearer shares (= shares in bearer form are owned by the person in whose possession the share certificates are; they are freely transferable, e.g. ordinary and preference shares in AG)
Stammaktien	ordinary shares [common stock/ common equity]
Stammkapital	share capital (in GmbH)
Vorzugsaktien	preference shares [preferred stock]
KAPITALRÜCKLAGE	CAPITAL RESERVE, primarily share premium account*
Agio	share premium
Aufgeld	share premium
GEWINNRÜCKLAGEN	REVENUE RESERVES (= reserves arising from retained profits)
andere Gewinnrücklagen	other revenue reserves
gesetzliche Rücklage	legal reserve (= reserve required by law, AktG)
Rücklage für eigene Anteile	reserve for own shares*

satzungsmäßige Rücklagen	reserves provided for by the articles of association* [statutory reserves]
GEWINNVORTRAG/VERLUSTVORTRAG	PROFIT AND LOSS ACCOUNT BROUGHT FORWARD (= previous years' profits and losses accumulated)
thesaurierte Gewinne	accumulated profits
JAHRESÜBERSCHUß/JAHRESFEHLBETRAG	PROFIT OR LOSS FOR THE FINANCIAL YEAR*
Jahresergebnis	annual result/profit or loss
BILANZGEWINN	BALANCE SHEET PROFIT
Einstellung in Gewinnrücklagen	transfer to revenue reserves
Dividende	dividends
KONZERNGEWINN	GROUP PROFIT [CONSOLIDATED RETAINED EARNINGS]
konsolidiertes Beteiligungsunternehmen	consolidated group undertaking
ANTEILE ANDERER GESELLSCHAFTER	MINORITY INTERESTS* (= minority shareholders' part in the consolidated capital and reserves)
ANTEILE IM FREMDBESITZ	MINORITY INTERESTS* (= minority shareholders' part in the consolidated capital and reserves)
andere Gesellschafter	minority shareholders
SONDERPOSTEN MIT RÜCKLAGEANTEIL	SPECIAL TAX-ALLOWABLE RESERVES
Wertberichtigungen zum Anlagevermögen	special additional depreciation on fixed assets (permitted by German tax law)
Wertberichtigungen zum Umlaufvermögen	special additional write-off on debtors (permitted by German tax law)
steuerfreie Rücklagen	tax-free reserves (profits transferred into these reserves are temporarily not taxed)
RÜCKSTELLUNGEN	PROVISIONS FOR LIABILITIES AND CHARGES [ACCRUALS]*
Rückstellungen für latente Steuern	provision for deferred taxation

Rückstellungen für Pensionen und ähnliche Verpflichtungen	provisions for pensions and similar obligations
Rückstellungen für Risiken aus schwebendenen Geschäften:	provisions for risks with contractual commitments:
• **Anlagenbau**	• plant building in progress (= long-term contract)
• **Bürgschaften**	• guarantees [guaranties]
• **Einkaufs- und Verkaufskontrakte**	• purchase and sales contracts
• **Schadensersatzansprüche**	• compensation claims
Rückstellungen für Steuern	tax provisions
Rückstellungen für ungewisse Verbindlichkeiten:	provisions for probable charges:
• **Aufwendungen für vorzeitige Pensionierung und Sozialplan**	• expenditure for early retirement and for social fund for employees
• **Boni**	• bonuses
• **Garantieverpflichtungen**	• guarantee obligations [guaranty obligations]
• **Jubiläumszuwendungen**	• anniversary gifts or awards to employees
• **Provisionen**	• commissions
• **Prozeßrückstellungen**	• provisions for litigation costs
• **Rabatte**	• rebates
• **soziale Abgaben**	• social benefits
• **Urlaubsentgelte, -gehälter**	• holiday payments [vacation pay]
sonstige Rückstellungen:	other provisions*:
• **austehende Rechnungen**	• accruals
• **Berufsgenossenschaftsbeiträge**	• contributions for occupational accident insurance
• **Garantieverpflichtungen**	• guarantee obligations [guaranty obligations]
• **Instandhaltung**	• repairs and maintenance
• **Jahresabschlußkosten**	• annual report preparation costs
• **Miet- und Leasingverpfichtungen**	• rent and leasing obligations
• **Personalkosten**	• staff costs
Steuerrückstellungen	tax provisions

versicherungstechnische Rückstellungen	provisions for insurances
VERBINDLICHKEITEN	CREDITORS [LIABILITIES/ ACCOUNTS PAYABLE]
Anleihen, davon konvertibel	debenture loans, of which convertible
erhaltene Anzahlungen auf Bestellungen	payments received on account of customer orders
Sicherheiten für Verbindlichkeiten:	securities for creditors [securities for liabilities]:
• **Grundpfandrechte**	• rights over land due to mortgages
• **Reallasten**	• mortgages
sonstige Verbindlichkeiten	other creditors [liabilities] of which
• **davon aus Steuern**	• for taxation
• **davon im Rahmen der sozialen Sicherheit**	• for social security
Verbindlichkeiten aus der Annahme gezogener Wechsel und der Ausstellung eigener Wechsel	(net) bills of exchange payable [liabilities on bills accepted and drawn]
Verbindlichkeiten aus Lieferungen und Leistungen	trade creditors* [trade payables]
Verbindlichkeiten gegenüber Kreditinstituten	bank loans and overdrafts*
Verbindlichkeiten gegenüber Unternehmen, mit denen ein Beteiligungsverhältnis besteht	amounts owed to undertakings in which the company has a participating interest* [payable to enterprises in which participations are held]
Verbindlichkeiten gegenüber verbundenen Unternehmen	amounts owed to group undertakings* [payable to affiliated enterprises]
Verbindlichkeiten mit einer Restlaufzeit bis zu einem Jahr	creditors [liabilities]: amounts falling due within one year*
Verbindlichkeiten mit einer Restlaufzeit von mehr als einem Jahr	creditors [liabilities]: amounts falling due after more than one year*
Verbindlichkeiten mit einer Restlaufzeit über fünf Jahre	creditors [liabilities]: amounts falling due after more than five years*
RECHNUNGSABGRENZUNGSPOSTEN	ACCRUALS AND DEFERRED INCOME*
Rechnungsabgrenzungsposten	sum total of all accruals and deferred income

41

4 Die Gewinn- und Verlustrechnung

The profit and loss account

Was ist die Gewinn- und Verlustrechnung?

Im vorigen Kapitel wurde bereits erwähnt, daß der Gewinn bzw. Verlust eines Geschäftsjahres auf der Passivseite einer Bilanz unter "Rücklagen" aufgenommen wird. Wenn man nun erfahren will, wie dieser Gewinn zustande gekommen ist, nimmt man sich die Gewinn- und Verlustrechnung vor, in der das finanzielle Ergebnis eines Geschäftsjahres kalkuliert wird.

Die Gewinn- und Verlustrechnung ist eine **Auflistung des Einkommens und der Ausgaben** einer Firma. Sie umfaßt einen festgelegten Zeitraum (das Rechnungsjahr), der mit dem in der Bilanz übereinstimmen muß. Ganz einfach betrachtet werden die gesamten Ausgaben von dem Gesamteinkommen abgezogen, um den Gewinn oder Verlust zu ermitteln. Wenn das Einkommen die Ausgaben übersteigt, zeigt die Erfolgsrechnung einen Gewinn. Wenn dagegen die Ausgaben die Einnahmen übersteigen, ergibt das einen Verlust.

Die Gewinn- und Verlustrechnung großer Kapitalgesellschaften muß in Deutschland gemäß einem Format aufgestellt werden, das vom Gesetzgeber vorgeschrieben ist (im HGB). Es gibt prinzipiell zwei Varianten des Formats:

- Schema 1 für das **produzierende Gewerbe** (also Industrie im engeren Sinne), und
- Schema 2 für das **nichtproduzierende Gewerbe** (Handel und Dienstleistungen).

Der augenfälligste Unterschied zwischen einem produzierenden und einem nichtproduzierenden Unternehmen ist, daß ein Hersteller Güter produziert und ein Nicht-Hersteller fertige Güter oder Dienstleistungen kauft und verkauft. Deshalb muß ein Hersteller in seiner Rechnungslegung zum Beispiel Rohstoffe miteinbeziehen, ein Posten, der in den Büchern einer Handelsfirma nicht auftaucht.

Das bedeutet, Schema 1 hat detailliertere Herstellungskosten, die dem Tätigkeitsbereich eines Herstellers entsprechen, also Einkauf von Material, Produktion von Gütern und Verkauf von Fertigwaren. Die Herstellungskosten solch einer Firma bestehen daher aus einer Reihe von Posten wie Materialkosten, Arbeitsaufwand, Maschinenbetrieb.

Ein Nicht-Hersteller, z.B. ein Händler, hat keine Herstellungskosten, und deshalb enthalten seine Kosten zur Erzielung der Umsatzerlöse nur die Kosten für den

Einkauf der Güter, die wieder verkauft werden sollen. Dies bedeutet eine vereinfachte Gewinn- und Verlustrechnung.

Abgesehen davon sind beide Schemata identisch.

Dieses Buch beschreibt nur Schema 1, weil es das kompliziertere von beiden ist. Ein weiterer Grund für die Betonung von Schema 1 ist, daß es in konsolidierten Jahresberichten fast ausschließlich zu finden ist. Das kommt daher, weil ein Konzern im Normalfall immer auch mindestens ein produzierendes Unternehmen enthält.

Der Aufbau einer deutschen Gewinn- und Verlustrechnung

1. Umsatzerlöse
2. Erhöhung oder Verminderung des Bestands an fertigen und unfertigen Erzeugnissen (Besfandsveränderungen)
3. Andere aktivierte Eigenleistungen
4. Sonstige betriebliche Erträge
5. Materialaufwand
6. Personalaufwand
7. Abschreibungen
8. Sonstige betriebliche Aufwendungen
9. Erträge aus Beteiligungen (Beteiligungsergebnis)
10. Erträge aus anderen Wertpapieren und Ausleihungen des Finanzanlagevermögens
11. Sonstige Zinsen und ähnliche Erträge
12. Abschreibungen auf Finanzanlagen und auf Wertpapiere des Umlaufvermögens
13. Zinsen und ähnliche Aufwendungen
14. Ergebnis der gewöhnlichen Geschäftstätigkeit
15. Außerordentliche Erträge
16. Außerordentliche Aufwendungen
17. Außerordentliches Ergebnis
18. Steuern vom Einkommen und vom Ertrag
19. Sonstige Steuern
20. Jahresüberschuß/Jahresfehlbetrag

(Schema 1 nach HGB)

Erklärungen zu den einzelnen Posten der Gewinn- und Verlustrechnung (Schema 1)

1. UMSATZERLÖSE

Hier handelt es sich einfach um Verkäufe, die während des Geschäftsjahres getätigt wurden.

2. BESTANDSVERÄNDERUNGEN/ERHÖHUNG ODER VERMINDERUNG DES BESTANDS AN FERTIGEN UND UNFERTIGEN ERZEUGNISSEN

Bestandsveränderungen sind einerseits Erhöhungen und andererseits Verminderungen des Bestandes. Ein Hersteller hat sowohl fertige als auch unfertige Erzeugnisse.

Eine Erhöhung liegt vor, wenn im Rechnungsjahr mehr Güter produziert als verkauft wurden und eine Verminderung, wenn weniger Güter produziert als verkauft wurden. Das letztere ist nur möglich, wenn ein Lagerbestand, der noch aus dem vorigen Abrechnungszeitraum stammt, in diesem Abrechnungszeitraum verkauft wurde.

3. ANDERE AKTIVIERTE EIGENLEISTUNGEN

Unter aktivierten Eigenleistungen versteht man Bestände mit einem bestimmten Zweck. Sie beinhalten hergestellte Fertigprodukte, die ein Unternehmen für den eigenen Betrieb verwendet. Mit anderen Worten, die Firma verkauft Fertigprodukte zu Herstellungskosten an sich selbst. Die Güter müssen "aktiviert" werden, das heißt, sie werden in das Vermögen der Firma integriert. Ein Beispiel dafür wäre, wenn eine Baufirma ihre eigenen Gebäude baut.

4. SONSTIGE BETRIEBLICHE ERTRÄGE

Ein Unternehmen hat oft Einkommensquellen, die am Rande ihrer gewöhnlichen Geschäftstätigkeit stehen, zum Beispiel Einkünfte aus dem Verkauf von Nebenprodukten.

5. MATERIALAUFWAND

Dieser Posten umfaßt die Kosten für Rohstoffe, Hilfs- und Betriebsstoffe, für extern eingekaufte Waren und Dienstleistungen eines Produktionsbetriebs.

6. PERSONALAUFWAND

Es gibt im Prinzip zwei Arten von Personalkosten:

- Löhne und Gehälter
- Sozialkosten, die unter anderem Sozialversicherungsbeiträge des Arbeitgebers beinhalten.

7. ABSCHREIBUNGEN

Es gibt Abschreibungen auf Sachanlagen wie Gebäude oder Maschinen, und Abschreibungen auf immaterielle Vermögensgegenstände wie Patente oder Geschäftswert. Beide Arten dienen demselben Zweck, nämlich dem Verteilen der Kosten eines Vermögensgegenstandes, der im allgemeinen teuer und beim Erwerb voll zu bezahlen ist, über die Nutzungsdauer. (Nähere Erklärungen dazu finden sich in Kapitel 5 über Anhang.)

8. SONSTIGE BETRIEBLICHE AUFWENDUNGEN

Dies sind Kosten, die zur gewöhnlichen Geschäftstätigkeit gehören, die aber nebenher anfallen, zum Beispiel Kursverluste bei Import/Exporttätigkeit, oder Pacht- und Versicherungskosten für das Betriebsgebäude.

9. ERTRÄGE AUS BETEILIGUNGEN/BETEILIGUNGSERGEBNIS

Beteiligungen sind im allgemeinen Aktienbestände bzw. Geschäftsanteile von mehr als 20%. Unter Erträgen aus Beteiligungen versteht man im Normalfall Dividende. Diese Erträge entstehen auch, wenn ein Unternehmen an einem anderen Unternehmen beteiligt ist und auf Grund eines Vertrags das Recht auf einen Anteil am Gewinn dieses Unternehmens hat. Man nennt diese Kontrakte Gewinnabführverträge.

10. ERTRÄGE AUS ANDEREN WERTPAPIEREN UND AUSLEIHUNGEN DES FINANZANLAGEVERMÖGENS

Dieser Posten beinhaltet sowohl Dividende aus kleinen Aktienbeständen bzw. Geschäftsanteilen (im allgemeinen weniger als 20%) als auch Zinserträge aus langfristigen Darlehen.

11. SONSTIGE ZINSEN UND ÄHNLICHE ERTRÄGE

Beispiele für diesen Posten sind erhaltene Bankzinsen für Sparguthaben oder Zinseinkommen von Privatdarlehen (das heißt an Privatpersonen gegebene Kredite). Dieser Posten und Posten 13 sind oft als **Zinsergebnis** zusammengefaßt.

12. ABSCHREIBUNGEN AUF FINANZANLAGEN UND WERTPAPIERE DES UMLAUFVERMÖGENS

Diese Abschreibungen werden auf Grund von Wertverlusten angesetzt. Wertverluste können bei allen Arten von Wertpapieranlagen entstehen. Beispiele dafür sind eine Wertminderung von Aktien an der Börse, die voraussichtlich von Dauer ist, und gegebene Darlehen, die voraussichtlich nicht in voller Höhe zurückgezahlt werden.

13. ZINSEN UND ÄHNLICHE AUFWENDUNGEN

Sie enthalten Kontoführungskosten, Überziehungskreditkosten, Zinsaufwendungen für erhaltene Darlehen und ähnliche Kosten. Dieser Posten und Posten 11 sind oft als **Zinsergebnis** zusammengefaßt.

14. ERGEBNIS DER GEWÖHNLICHEN GESCHÄFTSTÄTIGKEIT

Man kalkuliert diesen Posten, indem man die Geschäftsaufwendungen von den Geschäftserträgen subtrahiert. Diese Zahl wird sehr häufig für Analysen und zu Vergleichszwecken verwendet.

15. AUSSERORDENTLICHE ERTRÄGE

(siehe 17)

16. AUSSERORDENTLICHE AUFWENDUNGEN

(siehe 17)

17. AUSSERORDENTLICHES ERGEBNIS

Diese drei Posten entstehen durch Ereignisse, die außerhalb der gewöhnlichen Geschäftstätigkeit eines Unternehmens stehen (daher ihre Positionierung). Ein gutes Beispiel sind Feuer- und Diebstahlschäden.

18. STEUERN VOM EINKOMMEN UND VOM ERTRAG

(siehe 19)

19. SONSTIGE STEUERN

Das deutsche Steuerrecht umfaßt eine Vielzahl von Steuern, die oft mit den englischen Steuern nicht vergleichbar sind. Die beiden oben genannten Posten teilen die Steuern, die ein Unternehmen zu entrichten hat, in zwei grundsätzliche Bereiche ein.

Posten 18 beinhaltet die sogenannten Ertragsteuern, zu denen zum Beispiel die Körperschaftsteuer (Besteuerung des Geschäftsgewinns) gehört. Posten 19 umfaßt die sogenannten Substanzsteuern, die zum Beispiel auf Grund und Boden erhoben werden, sowie andere Steuern, wie z.B. Kraftfahrzeugsteuer und Umsatzsteuer.

20. JAHRESÜBERSCHUß/JAHRESFEHLBETRAG

Darunter versteht man den sogenannten "Nettogewinn bzw. -verlust", da es sich um den Gewinn nach Abzug aller Kosten handelt. Der Reingewinn kann an die Anteilseigner verteilt bzw. in die Rücklagen eingestellt werden. Wenn ein Verlust entsteht, kann er durch bestehende Gewinnrücklagen gedeckt werden.

What is the profit and loss account?

As seen in Chapter 3 on balance sheets, the profit or loss for the current year is listed as part of share capital on the capital and liabilities side, but this does not tell us anything about how the result has been arrived at. The detailed calculation of this result is found in the profit and loss account.

The profit and loss account is a **listing of income and expenditure** of a business. It covers a specified time period (the financial year) which has to be the same as the one covered in the balance sheet. In its simplest form the total expenditure is deducted from the total income in order to arrive at a profit or loss. If income exceeds expenditure, the account shows a profit. If expenditure exceeds income, the account shows a loss.

The profit and loss account of large companies must be presented according to a format prescribed by German legislation (set out in the HGB). There are two such formats:

- Format 1 for **manufacturing businesses**, and
- Format 2 for **non-manufacturing businesses** (e.g. retailing and services).

The most obvious difference between a manufacturing and a non-manufacturing business is that a manufacturer produces goods and a non-manufacturer buys and sells finished goods or services. Therefore a manufacturing business needs to account for the cost of buying, for example, raw materials, an item which would not appear in a non-manufacturing business's accounts.

Format 1 has a more detailed 'cost of sales' section which corresponds to the activities of a manufacturing business, i.e. buying materials, manufacturing products and selling finished goods. The 'cost of sales' of such a business is made up of a number of items such as the cost of raw materials, production labour, machines (in operation).

A non-manufacturer such as a retailer does not have any manufacturing expenses and therefore the cost of sales contains only the cost of buying the goods that the firm intends to sell. This means a simplified profit and loss account.

Apart from that the two formats are identical.

This book gives a detailed description of Format 1 only since it is the more complicated of the two. Another reason for emphasising Format 1 is that it is almost always found in consolidated accounts. This arises because groups usually contain at least one manufacturing business.

The structure of a German profit and loss account

1. Turnover*
2. Increase or decrease in stocks of finished goods and in work-in-progress
3. Own work capitalised*
4. Other operating income*
5. Cost of materials
6. Staff costs*
7. Depreciation
8. Other operating charges*
9. (Net) income from investments in other undertakings
10. Income from other investments and long-term loans
11. Other interest receivable and similar income
12. Amounts written off short-term and long-term investments
13. Interest payable and similar charges*
14. Profit or loss on ordinary activities
15. Extraordinary income*
16. Extraordinary charges*
17. Extraordinary profit or loss*
18. Taxes on profit
19. Other taxes
20. Profit or loss for the year

(Format 1 according to HGB)

Explanations of the individual headings of a profit and loss account (Format 1)

1. TURNOVER*

This represents sales made within one accounting period.

2. INCREASE OR DECREASE IN STOCKS OF FINISHED GOODS AND IN WORK-IN-PROGRESS/STOCK CHANGES

This is the so-called stock adjustment. A manufacturer has both work-in-progress and finished goods in stock. There is an increase in stock if more goods were produced than sold and a decrease in stock if fewer goods were produced than sold in the accounting period. The latter is only possible if stock left over from the previous accounting period was sold in the current accounting period.

3. OWN WORK CAPITALISED*

This also represents stock, but stock with a special purpose. It comprises manufactured goods which a business uses for its own purposes. Thus the goods are capitalised which means they are reclassified as fixed assets. The business makes a sale to itself at cost price. An example for this would be a construction business building its own premises.

4. OTHER OPERATING INCOME*

A business may have sources of income which are incidental to its main activity, for example, income from the sale of by-products.

5. COST OF MATERIALS

This section comprises the cost of raw materials, consumables, of externally purchased goods and services for a manufacturing business.

6. STAFF COSTS*

There are two groups of staff costs:

- wages and salaries
- social security and pension costs which cover among other things National Insurance contributions.

7. DEPRECIATION

Depreciation is calculated on tangible assets like buildings or machines, and on intangible assets like patents or goodwill in which case it is called amortisation. Both have the same purpose namely to spread the cost of an asset, generally large and payable in full at the time of purchase, over the number of years during which a business benefits from its use. (For a detailed explanation see Chapter 5 on Notes to the Financial Statements.)

8. OTHER OPERATING CHARGES*

These are expenses which are part of the business's normal trading activity but which are usually incidental, e.g. losses in foreign exchange transactions or lease and insurance costs for buildings.

9. INCOME FROM INVESTMENTS IN OTHER UNDERTAKINGS/NET INCOME FROM INVESTMENTS IN OTHER UNDERTAKINGS

Under this heading we find investments such as shareholdings in other companies (generally of more than 20%). Income from these shares normally constitutes dividends. Another type of investment income arises when a business part-owns another business (e.g. a partnership) and a contract entitles the business to a proportion of that other business's profits. Such an entitlement is based on a so-called profit transfer contract.

10. INCOME FROM OTHER INVESTMENTS AND LONG-TERM LOANS

This represents dividend income from small shareholdings (generally of less than 20%) and interest income from long-term loans.

11. OTHER INTEREST RECEIVABLE AND SIMILAR INCOME

Examples for this are bank interest received on monies held in a deposit account or interest income from private loans (loans made to individuals). This entry and entry 13 are often summarised as **net interest**.

12. AMOUNTS WRITTEN OFF LONG-TERM AND SHORT-TERM INVESTMENTS

This arises when there is a diminution in value of any type of investment. Examples are a drop in value of shares on the stock exchange which is expected to be permanent, and loan stock which is not expected to be paid back at the full rate.

13. INTEREST PAYABLE AND SIMILAR CHARGES*

This comprises bank account charges, bank overdraft interest charges, loan interest payable and similar items. This entry and entry 11 are often summarised as **net interest**.

14. PROFIT OR LOSS ON ORDINARY ACTIVITIES

The profit or loss on ordinary activities is arrived at by deducting trading expenditure from trading income. This figure is widely used for analysis and comparisons.

15. EXTRAORDINARY INCOME*

(see 17)

16. EXTRAORDINARY CHARGES*

(see 17)

17. EXTRAORDINARY PROFIT OR LOSS* (i.e. extraordinary income less extraordinary charges)

Events giving rise to the above three entries in the profit and loss account are outside a business's ordinary activities (hence its position). A good example would be fire and theft damages. (Please note that in the United Kingdom extraordinary items are more narrowly defined.)

18. TAXES ON PROFIT

(see 19)

19. OTHER TAXES

German legislation provides for a variety of taxes some of which are not directly comparable to British taxes. Suffice to say in this context: entry 18 comprises all taxes directly related to income, e.g. corporation tax (tax on business profit), and entry 19 contains the so-called 'substance taxes', e.g. tax on land, as well as other taxes, e.g. road tax and value-added tax.

20. PROFIT OR LOSS FOR THE YEAR

This is the so-called 'net profit or loss' as it is the profit after all business expenses. The net profit is available for distribution or for transfer to reserves. If the result is a loss, the amount may be covered by existing reserves.

Die Posten der Gewinn- und Verlustrechnung: Deutsch—Englisch

Profit and loss account entries: German—English

This chapter represents a **bilingual presentation of a profit and loss account** following the structure of real-life German profit and loss accounts. The entries under each heading are listed in alphabetical order to make reference easier.

As a profit and loss account is generally read in conjunction with the notes to the financial statements we have included terminology from these notes under the respective profit and loss account headings.

UMSATZERLÖSE	TURNOVER* (SALES)
andere Erlöse	sundry sales
Mieteinnahmen	rental income
Lizenzerträge	income from licences
BESTANDSVERÄNDERUNGEN UND ANDERE AKTIVIERTE EIGENLEISTUNGEN	CHANGE (i.e. increase or decrease) IN STOCKS OF FINISHED GOODS AND IN WORK-IN-PROGRESS*, AND OWN WORK CAPITALISED* [INCREASE OR DECREASE IN FINISHED INVENTORIES AND IN WORK-IN-PROCESS, AND CAPITALIZED IN-HOUSE OUTPUT]
andere aktivierte Eigenleistungen	own work capitalised* [other capitalized in-house output]
Erhöhungen des Bestands an fertigen und unfertigen Erzeugnissen	increase in stocks of finished goods and in work-in-progress [increase in finished inventories and in work-in-process]

Erhöhung des Bestands an unverrechneten Lieferungen und Leistungen	increase in goods and services (accounts) not balanced off
Verminderung des Bestands an fertigen und unfertigen Erzeugnissen	decrease in stocks of finished goods and in work-in-progress [decrease in finished inventories and in work-in-process]

SONSTIGE BETRIEBLICHE ERTRÄGE   OTHER OPERATING INCOME*

Erlöse aus Nebengeschäften	income from secondary/minor business activities
Erträge aus dem Abgang von Gegenständen des Anlagevermögens	profit on the disposal of (any type of) fixed assets
Erträge aus dem Abgang von Gegenständen des Sachanlagevermögens	profit on the disposal of tangible fixed assets
Erträge aus der Auflösung von Rückstellungen	income from the reversal [writing back] of provisions
Erträge aus der Auflösung von Rückstellungen für sonstige Steuern	income from the reversal [writing back] of provisions for other taxes
Erträge aus der Auflösung von Sonderposten mit Rücklageanteil	income from the reversal [writing back] of previous transfers to special tax-allowable reserves
Erträge aus der Herabsetzung von Forderungswertberichtigungen und dem Eingang ausgebuchter Forderungen	income from the reduction in doubtful debt provision and from the recovery [writing back] of bad debts previously written off
Erträge aus Dienstleistungen	income from services
Erträge aus Lizenzen	income from licences
Fremdwährungskursgewinne	exchange rate gains on foreign currencies
Gewinne aus dem Verkauf von Beteiligungen	profit on the sale of shares
Gewinne aus dem Verkauf von Sachanlagen	profit on the sale of tangible fixed assets
übrige betriebliche Erträge	sundry operating income
Währungs- und Kursgewinne	gains on foreign exchange transactions (= gains from exchange rate fluctuations)

Zuschüsse und Zulagen für Forschung und Entwicklung	contributions and grants for research and development

MATERIALAUFWAND	**COST OF MATERIALS**
Aufwendungen für bezogene Leistungen	cost of purchased/bought-in services
Aufwendungen für bezogene Waren	cost of purchased/bought-in goods
Aufwendungen für Roh-, Hilfs- und Betriebsstoffe	raw materials and consumables*
Betriebsstoffe	consumables
übrige Aufwendungen für Roh-, Hilfs- und Betriebsstoffe	other costs of raw materials and consumables
versicherungstechnische Aufwendungen	insurance costs

PERSONALAUFWAND	**STAFF COSTS* (PERSONNEL EXPENSES)**
Aufwendungen für Altersversorgung	pension costs
Aufwendungen für Unterstützung	other social costs
Löhne und Gehälter	wages and salaries*
soziale Abgaben	social security costs*

ABSCHREIBUNGEN	**DEPRECIATION**
Abschreibungen auf immaterielle Vermögensgegenstände	amortisation of intangible (fixed) assets
Abschreibungen auf immaterielle Vermögensgegenstände des Anlagevermögens und Sachanlagen sowie auf aktivierte Aufwendungen für die Ingangsetzung und Erweiterung des Geschäftsbetriebs	amortisation/depreciation of intangible and tangible fixed assets, as well as amortisation of set-up and business expansion costs capitalised
Abschreibungen auf Sachanlagen	depreciation of tangible fixed assets
außerplanmäßige Abschreibungen	exceptional depreciation charges (in excess of the normal depreciation charges)
planmäßige Abschreibungen	normal/scheduled depreciation
steuerliche Sonderabschreibungen	special depreciation required or permitted by German tax legislation (in excess of the normal depreciation charges)

SONSTIGE BETRIEBLICHE AUFWENDUNGEN	OTHER OPERATING CHARGES*
Bankspesen	bank charges
Beiträge an Berufsvertretungen	contributions to professional bodies and associations
Betriebsaufwendungen	operating charges
Bildung von Rückstellungen	creation of provisions
Bürobedarf	stationery, office supplies
Einstellungen in Sonderposten mit Rücklageanteil	transfers to special tax-allowable reserve
Forderungsausfälle	bad debts (written off) [loss of receivables outstanding]
freiwillige soziale Aufwendungen	voluntary expenditure for staff (= fringe benefits)
Gewerbekapitalsteuer	tax on assets (except land) levied by local government (= similar to UK council taxes)
Grundsteuer	tax on land levied by local government (= similar to UK council taxes)
Instandhaltungskosten	repair and maintenance costs
Mieten	rents
Pachten	leases
Personalnebenkosten	staff costs additional to employee remuneration (= employers' contributions and voluntary social costs)
Porto und Telefonkosten	postage and telephone costs
Provisionen	commissions
Reiseaufwendungen	travel expenses
Reisekosten	travel expenses
Sachkosten für Geschäftsräume	fixtures and fittings
Sachkosten für Personalausbildung	incidental costs for staff training
sonstige Gemeinkosten	sundry overheads
sonstige Steuern	other taxes

übrige Aufwendungen	sundry expenses
übrige betriebliche Aufwendungen	sundry operating charges
Verkaufsprovisionen	sales commission
Verluste aus dem Abgang von Gegenständen des Anlagevermögens	losses on the disposal of (any type of) fixed assets
Verluste aus Wertminderungen und der Ausbuchung von Forderungen	losses from doubtful and bad debts (= expected losses from probable and certain non-payment of debtors)
Vermögensteuer	tax on assets
Versicherungen	insurances
Vertriebsaufwendungen	distribution costs* (= selling expenses)
Verwaltungsaufwendungen	administrative expenses*
Verwaltungs- und Vertriebskosten	administrative expenses and distribution costs
Währungs- und Kursverluste	losses on foreign exchange transactions (= losses from exchange rate fluctuations)
Werbekosten	advertising costs (= marketing and advertising)

BETEILIGUNGSERGEBNIS	NET INCOME FROM INVESTMENTS IN OTHER UNDERTAKINGS
andere Beteiligungsaufwendungen	other charges related to investments in shares
Aufwendungen aus Verlustübernahmen	loss transfers
Ergebnis aus assoziierten Unternehmen	result (= net total of profit and loss transfers) from investments in associated undertakings
Erträge aus Beteiligungen	income from participating interests (= dividends and similar income)
Erträge aus Beteiligungen an verbundenen Unternehmen	income from shares in group undertakings* [income from shares in affiliated enterprises] (=dividends and similar income)
Erträge aus Gewinnabführverträgen	income from profit transfer contracts
Erträge aus Gewinnübernahmen	income from profit transfers

ERTRÄGE AUS ANDEREN WERTPAPIEREN UND AUSLEIHUNGEN DES FINANZANLAGEVERMÖGENS	INCOME FROM OTHER INVESTMENTS AND LONG-TERM LOANS
davon aus verbundenenen, nicht konsolidierten Unternehmen	of which from non-consolidated subsidiary undertakings
Kursgewinne bei Wertpapieren	exchange rate gains with investments
ABSCHREIBUNGEN AUF FINANZANLAGEN UND AUF WERTPAPIERE DES UMLAUFVERMÖGENS	AMOUNTS WRITTEN OFF FIXED-ASSET INVESTMENTS (= long-term) AND CURRENT ASSET INVESTMENTS (= short-term) [WRITE-DOWN OF FINANCIAL ASSETS AND SHORT-TERM INVESTMENTS]
Abschreibungen auf Finanzanlagen	amounts written off investments
ZINSEN UND ÄHNLICHE ERTRÄGE/ AUFWENDUNGEN	INTEREST AND SIMILAR INCOME/CHARGES (see net interest)
ZINSERTRÄGE/ZINSAUFWENDUNGEN	INTEREST RECEIVABLE/PAYABLE (see net interest)
ZINSERGEBNIS	NET INTEREST (= interest receivable less interest payable)
sonstige Zinsen und ähnliche Erträge	other interest receivable and similar income*
Zinsaufwendungen	interest payable
Zinsen und ähnliche Aufwendungen	interest payable and similar charges*
Zinserträge	interest receivable
ERGEBNIS DER GEWÖHNLICHEN GESCHÄFTSTÄTIGKEIT	PROFIT OR LOSS ON ORDINARY ACTIVITIES
Jahresergebnis	annual result
AUßERORDENTLICHE ERTRÄGE	EXTRAORDINARY INCOME*
Verkauf einer Filiale	sale of a branch

AUßERORDENTLICHE AUFWENDUNGEN	EXTRAORDINARY CHARGES*
Aufwendungen für Schließungen	closure costs
AUßERORDENTLICHES ERGEBNIS	EXTRAORDINARY PROFIT OR LOSS*
Veräußerung von Geschäftsanteilen	sale of shareholdings
STEUERN VOM EINKOMMEN UND VOM ERTRAG	TAXES ON PROFIT [TAXES ON INCOME]
Auflösung Steuerrückstellungen	reversal [writing back] of tax provisions
Ertragsteueraufwand	cost of all taxes on profit [taxes on income] (= corporation tax, local government tax on profits, tax on investment income)
Erstattungen für Vorjahre	tax refunds for previous years
Gewerbeertragsteuer	tax on profits levied by local government (= similar to UK council taxes)
Kapitalertragsteuer	tax on investment income [capital yields tax] (= tax on dividends, interest, etc.)
Körperschaftsteuer	corporation tax [corporate tax/ corporation income tax] (= tax on business profits)
latente Steuern	deferred tax
Steuergutschriften	tax credits
SONSTIGE STEUERN	OTHER TAXES
Ausfuhrzölle	customs duty on exports
Gewerbekapitalsteuer	tax on assets (except land) levied by local government (= similar to UK council taxes)
Grundsteuer	tax on land levied by local government (= similar to UK council taxes)
Kraftfahrzeugsteuer	road tax

Mineralölsteuer	mineral oil tax
Umsatzsteuer	value-added tax
Vermögensteuer	tax on assets
Versicherungsteuer	tax on insurances
Wechselsteuer	tax on bills of exchange
JAHRESÜBERSCHUß/ JAHRESFEHLBETRAG	PROFIT OR LOSS FOR THE YEAR [NET INCOME OR NET LOSS FOR THE YEAR]
Anteile Konzernfremder am Jahresergebnis	minority interests in the profit or loss for the current year (= minority shareholders' part in the consolidated profit or loss)
auf konzernfremde Gesellschafter entfallender Verlust	loss attributable to minority interests (i.e. minority shareholders)
konzernfremden Gesellschaftern zustehender Gewinn	profit attributable to minority interests (i.e. minority shareholders)

5 Der Anhang

The notes to the financial statements

Was ist der Anhang?

Der Anhang enthält im wesentlichen Pflichtangaben und Erläuterungen zu Bilanz und Gewinn- und Verlustrechnung. Daher ist er inhaltlich fest mit diesen verbunden. Es gibt gesetzliche Vorschriften, die bestimmte Erläuterungen zu Einzelpositionen (der Bilanz und Erfolgsrechnung) und gewisse Pflichtangaben ausdrücklich verlangen. Das deutsche Gesetz erlaubt allerdings auch freiwillige Zusatzangaben, z.B. Graphen, die der Veranschaulichung dienen.

Der Anhang enthält:

1 eine **Untergliederung der Posten in der Bilanz und der Gewinn- und Verlustrechnung.**

Ein Beispiel wäre die Unterteilung von Sachanlagen. Es finden sich hier auch noch weitere Informationen, z.B. Zugänge und Abgänge von Sachanlagen während des Geschäftsjahres oder Informationen über Bürgschaften. (Ausführliche Angaben dazu in der zweisprachigen Darstellung der Kapitel 3 und 4.)

2 zusätzliche **Erläuterungen und Informationen zu Rechnungsgrundsätzen und -methoden.**

Diese Rechnungsgrundsätze und -methoden bilden die Kalkulationsbasis für den Jahresabschluß. Außerdem enthält dieser Teil zusätzlich Informationen über finanzielle Gegebenheiten, die nicht aus der Bilanz oder der Gewinn- und Verlustrechnung ersichtlich sind, die jedoch für Interessierte von Wichtigkeit sind.

Zu diesen Angaben im Anhang gehören, nicht immer in derselben Reihenfolge:

a. Konsolidierungsgrundsätze/Konsolidierungsmethoden

Wenn zu einem Unternehmen mehrere Firmen gehören, ist für die Aktionäre oder potentiellen Anleger nicht nur von Bedeutung, wie die einzelnen Firmen wirtschaften, sondern auch, wie der Gesamtkonzern (d.h. die Gruppe von Firmen) finanziell dasteht.

Zu diesem Zweck werden die Jahresabschlüsse der einzelnen Firmen "konsolidiert", d.h. zusammengefaßt. Es gibt verschiedene Methoden der

Konsolidierung, je nachdem, wie hoch der Kapitalanteil bzw. die Stimmrechte an den einzelnen Firmen sind.

Ein Beispiel: Eine Muttergesellschaft hat an ihrer Tochtergesellschaft einen Kapitalanteil von 100%. Die Tochtergesellschaft hat ein Beteiligungsverhältnis mit einer dritten Firma mit 25% Kapitalanteil mit Stimmrechten. Folglich hat die Muttergesellschaft auch einen Anteil an der dritten Firma. Dieser Konzern besteht dann aus drei Firmen und benötigt zwei verschiedene Konsolidierungsmethoden wegen der zwei verschiedenen Beteiligungen (100 bzw. 25%).

b. Bilanzierungs- und Bewertungsgrundsätze

Diese beinhalten Grundsätze der Bewertung von einzelnen Positionen der Bilanz und Erfolgsrechnung, unter anderem Abschreibungsmethoden und Bewertung von Vorräten.

Die **Abschreibung** ist eine Methode der zeitlichen Verteilung der Anschaffungskosten eines Anlageguts. Abgeschrieben werden z.B. Maschinen, Fahrzeuge, d.h. Güter, die im Abrechnungszeitraum (der ja normalerweise ein Jahr beträgt) nicht verbraucht werden, die jedoch über die Zeit hinweg an Wert verlieren. Die Firma muß einen bestimmten Wertverlust pro Jahr veranschlagen und diesen vom Anschaffungswert bzw. vom Wert des Vorjahres absetzen. In der Bilanz erscheint also dasselbe Gut jedes Jahr mit einem geringeren Wert, dem sogenannten Buchwert. Die Abschreibungshöhe richtet sich nach der voraussichtlichen Nutzungsdauer. Abschreibungen werden immer auf der Aktivseite der Bilanz durchgeführt. In der Gewinn- und Verlustrechnung werden die Abschreibungen als Aufwendungen angeführt.

Es werden vorwiegend zwei Verfahren der Abschreibung angewendet.

- **Die lineare Abschreibung.** Sie verrechnet gleichbleibende Jahresbeträge, z.B. 10% pro Jahr oder über 10 Jahre, 25% pro Jahr oder über 4 Jahre.
- **Die degressive Abschreibung.** Sie verrechnet fallende Jahresbeträge, z.B. 200 DM (Jahr 1), 160 DM (Jahr 2), 130 DM (Jahr 3).

c. Währungsumrechnungsprinzipien

Fremdwährungsumrechnung findet sich nur in Konzernjahresberichten. Die Zahlen in den ausländischen Jahresberichten werden in die einheimische Währung umgerechnet.

Wichtig sind bei all den genannten Punkten vor allem die Erklärung und Begründung von Änderungen der Methoden und Prinzipien gegenüber dem Vorjahr.

What are the notes to the financial statements?

The notes to the financial statements give further details to balance sheet and profit and loss account and are therefore an integral part of the annual report.

According to German company law certain details must be present in the notes. But it also allows the inclusion of further details which a company can add on a voluntary basis, e.g. charts or diagrams which provide more clarity.

The notes provide:

1 details on the **break-down of figures in both balance sheet and profit and loss account.**

   For example, you find subdivisions of tangible fixed assets in this section of the notes. Also purchases and sales of assets or defaults on guarantees are listed here. (For further details and examples please refer to the bilingual listings of Chapters 3 and 4.)

2 additional **explanations and information on accounting principles.**

   These accounting principles form the basis of calculation for the annual report. Furthermore this section contains additional information on financial circumstances which cannot be deduced from the balance sheet and profit and loss account but which are very important for interested parties.

The details provided in this section of the notes are primarily the following:

a. Basis of consolidation

One business may consist of several companies (e.g. clothes manufacture and cloth production). The shareholders and potential investors are of course interested in the financial affairs of each individual company, one may do well and another may make losses. However, it is also important to know how the group of companies as a whole performs.

In order to determine the overall performance of a group of companies the financial statements of individual member companies are 'consolidated', i.e. combined or summarised. There are different methods of consolidation depending on the percentage of shares and/or voting rights in a company owned by another.

For example, Company A has a 100% shareholding in Company B: A is the parent undertaking and B its subsidiary. The subsidiary itself holds 25% of the shares and voting rights in Company C. Therefore the parent undertaking also has a share in Company C. Thus the group consists of three companies. Two different methods of consolidation are necessary because of the two different shareholdings (100% and 25%).

b. Accounting policies

Accounting policies are the basic principles applied when calculating balance sheet and profit and loss account figures. Two major policies are depreciation and valuation of stock.

Depreciation is the allocation of the cost of an asset over the period of time the business expects to use this asset, e.g. a machine or a motor vehicle. These assets are normally in use for more than one accounting period (which is usually a year). Every year the company has to account for a certain amount of use. The most appropriate depreciation method is chosen, a figure calculated and incorporated into the financial statements. On the one hand, depreciation is a yearly cost in the profit and loss account, and on the other, depreciation is deducted from the original cost in the first year and the so-called book value in subsequent years in the balance sheet (book value = cost minus depreciation). For that reason the same asset has a lower value in the current balance sheet than in the previous one. Please note that the depreciation of assets is always found in the fixed asset section of the balance sheet. In the profit and loss account depreciation is stated as a cost.

There are two main bases for depreciation:

- **The straight-line basis**. Depreciation calculated on the straight-line basis shows the same charge each year, e.g. 10% p.a. or equally over 10 years, 25% p.a. or equally over 4 years.
- **The reducing-balance basis**. Depreciation calculated on the reducing-balance basis results in a reduced charge each year, e.g. 200 DM (year 1), 160 DM (year 2), 130 DM (year 3).

c. Currency translation principles

Foreign currency translation arises only in group accounts. The figures in the foreign currency accounts are translated into the 'home' currency.

With any of the above notes, particular attention has to be paid to changes in accounting policies since the previous year and the reasons and justifications for these alterations.

Beispiele
Examples

The following is a list of representative examples from the above mentioned headings of the notes. These include individual terms as well as sentences.

Konsolidierungsgrundsätze

Basis of consolidation

1. Buchwert des Eigenkapitals/Buchwertmethode
2. Verschmelzung
3. konzerninterne Lieferungen
4. Innenumsatzerlöse
5. Verrechnung mit den Konzerngewinnrücklagen
6. Zwischenabschluß
7. das Stammkapital
8. die Vermögens- und Ertragslage
9. Anteile in Fremdbesitz
10. Forderungen und Verbindlichkeiten zwischen den konsolidierten Gesellschaften werden gegeneinander aufgerechnet.
11. Das Bilanzergebnis wird in gleicher Höhe ausgewiesen.
12. Gegenüber dem Vorjahr sind drei Auslandsgesellschaften erstmals konsolidiert worden.
13. Das Geschäftsjahr aller konsolidierten Gesellschaften ist das Kalenderjahr.
14. Die Einzelabschlüsse der Tochterunternehmen wurden nach konzerneinheitlichen Bilanzierungs- und Bewertungsmethoden erstellt.
15. Alle Abschlüsse entsprechen den Grundsätzen ordnungsmäßiger Buchführung.
16. Im Konsolidierungskreis haben sich gegenüber dem Vorjahr folgende Änderungen ergeben.

17. Die Gesellschaft wurde liquidiert.
18. die Tochterunternehmen, bei denen der Muttergesellschaft mehr als 50% der Stimmrechte zustehen.
19. Von der Möglichkeit einer anteilsmäßigen Konsolidierung wird kein Gebrauch gemacht.
20. Alle einbezogenen Abschlüsse sind auf den gleichen Stichtag erstellt. Sie werden von unabhängigen Abschlußprüfern geprüft und testiert.
21. Wertberichtigungen und Abschreibungen auf Forderungen aus Einzelabschlüssen, die aufgrund der Konsolidierung frei geworden sind, werden dem Jahresergebnis gutgebracht.
22. Die Umsatzerlöse enthalten nur Umsätze mit Kunden außerhalb des Konsolidierungskreises.
23. Zwischenergebnisse, konzerninterne Umsätze, Aufwendungen und Erträge sowie alle Forderungen und Verbindlichkeiten zwischen konsolidierten Gesellschaften werden eliminiert.

Bilanzierungs- und Bewertungsgrundsätze

Accounting policies

1. unverrechnete Lieferungen und Leistungen
2. niedrig verzinsliche langfristige Ausleihungen
3. Wiederbeschaffungs- bzw. Wiederherstellungskosten
4. vernünftige kaufmännische Beurteilung
5. zeitlich begrenzte Unterschiede zwischen handels- und steuerrechtlicher Gewinnermittlung
6. Einzel- und Pauschalwertberichtigungen
7. niedrigere Börsenkurse
8. das bewegliche Sachanlagevermögen
9. geringwertige Anlagegegenstände
10. steuerliche Möglichkeiten zur Sonderabschreibung
11. mit einem Abschreibungssatz von 20 Prozent belegen
12. die Laufzeit der Mietverträge
13. der Wertansatz der übrigen Rückstellungen
14. Immaterielle Vermögensgegenstände werden zu Anschaffungskosten und in längstens fünf Jahren abgeschrieben.
15. Einen Goodwill verrechnen wir mit den Gewinnrücklagen.
16. Die Herstellungskosten umfassen Fertigungsmaterial, Fertigungslöhne sowie Material- und Fertigungsgemeinkosten.

17. Bei der Bemessung der Rückstellungen haben wir allen erkennbaren Risiken angemessen und ausreichend Rechnung getragen.
18. Aktivische und passivische Abgrenzungen werden zusammengefaßt.
19. Gegenstände des Sachanlagevermögens werden entsprechend ihrer voraussichtlichen wirtschaftlichen Nutzungsdauer abgeschrieben.
20. Im Ausland wird überwiegend linear abgeschrieben.
21. Finanzanlagen werden mit ihren Anschaffungswerten bilanziert.
22. Die Herstellungskosten werden überwiegend mit Hilfe der Durchschnittsmethode ermittelt.
23. Abschreibungen wegen allgemeiner und besonderer Kreditrisiken
24. Als Nutzungsdauer wurde die jeweilige betriebsgewöhnliche Nutzungsdauer angewandt.
25. Die Bewertung der Vorräte erfolgte zum Einstandswert.
26. Verbindlichkeiten wurden zum Nennwert angesetzt.
27. Es wird mit den steuerlich zulässigen Höchstsätzen degressiv abgeschrieben.
28. Dem allgemeinen Kreditrisiko wird durch eine Pauschalwertberichtigung angemessen Rechnung getragen.
29. Die Wertansätze der Eventualverbindlichkeiten entsprechen dem am Bilanztag bestehenden Haftungsumfang.
30. Bei assoziierten Unternehmen werden deren Bewertungsmethoden übernommen.
31. Geringwertige Wirtschaftsgüter werden im Zugangsjahr voll abgeschrieben.
32. Ersatzteile und sonstige Roh-, Hilfs- und Betriebsstoffe werden zu Durchschnittspreisen bewertet.
33. Wertpapiere sind zu Anschaffungskosten angesetzt.
34. Die Pensionsrückstellungen sind mit dem vollen Deckungsbetrag angesetzt.
35. Verbindlichkeiten sind mit dem Rückzahlungsbetrag passiviert.

Währungsumrechnungsprinzipien

Currency translation principles

1. der Anschaffungskurs
2. der Jahresdurchschnittskurs des jeweiligen Anschaffungsjahres = der historische Kurs
3. der Mittelkurs am Bilanzstichtag
4. Die Aufwendungen und Erträge in der Gewinn- und Verlustrechnung rechnen wir zum Jahresdurchschnittskurs um.

5. Einen Umrechnungsverlust buchen wir zu Lasten des Jahresergebnisses.

6. Ein Umrechnungsgewinn wird einer Rückstellung für Währungsrisiken zugeführt.

7. Währungsrisiken, die sich aus der Anwendung verschiedener Kurse in der Gewinn- und Verlustrechnung ergeben, werden in "sonstige betriebliche Aufwendungen" eingestellt.

8. Geldbestände und Bankguthaben in fremder Währung werden zum Geldkurs am Bilanzstichtag umgerechnet.

9. Umrechnungsdifferenzen werden bei den Gewinnrücklagen berücksichtigt.

10. Forderungen und Verbindlichkeiten werden zu den Kursen zum Zeitpunkt des Geschäftsvorfalls bewertet.

6 Selbstüberprüfung

Self-testing exercises

Übungen
Exercises

A. Under which heading of the balance sheet would you find the following entries?

1. Beteiligungen
2. Dividende
3. gesetzliche Rücklagen
4. Konzessionen
5. Stammaktien
6. Jahresabschlußkosten
7. Forderungen aus dem Versicherungsgeschäft
8. Halbfertige Erzeugnisse

B. Under which heading of the profit and loss account would you find the following entries?

1. Körperschaftsteuer
2. Mieteinnahmen
3. Währungs- und Kursgewinne
4. Vermögensteuer
5. Erträge aus Lizenzen
6. Betriebsstoffe
7. Reisekosten
8. Währungs- und Kursverluste

C. Please choose the correct answer.

1. Welcher der folgenden Posten findet sich nicht auf der Aktivseite der Bilanz?
   a Technische Anlagen und Maschinen
   b Personalkosten – Verbindlichkeit
   c Geschäfts- und Firmenwert
   d Forderungen aus Lieferungen und Leistungen

2. Welcher der folgenden Posten findet sich nicht auf der Passivseite der Bilanz?
   a Disagio
   b Anleihen
   c Urlaubsgehälter – Rückstellung
   d Verbindlichkeiten

3. Für einen Nähmaschinenhersteller ist eine Nähmaschine
   a eine Finanzanlage
   b eine technische Anlage
   c eine Sachanlage
   d ein Fertigerzeugnis?

4. Für einen Kleidungshersteller ist eine Nähmaschine
   a Kapital
   b eine technische Anlage
   c eine Rückstellung
   d ein Gegenstand des Anlagevermögens?

D. Please explain and/or define the following terms.

1. Was versteht man unter "Abgrenzungsposten"?
2. Erklären Sie den Unterschied zwischen Anlage- und Umlaufvermögen!
3. Gehören Rückstellungen zum Eigenkapital oder zum Fremdkapital? Warum?
4. Was versteht man unter degressiver Abschreibung? Warum wird Abschreibung angewandt?
5. Was versteht man unter "Buchwert"?
6. Was bedeutet Konsolidierung?
7. Was sind immaterielle Vermögensgegenstände?

E. Please translate the following sentences.

1. In calculating depreciation it is necessary to know
   a the original cost of the fixed asset
   b the probable period of use of the asset
   c the probable trade-in or scrap value of the asset at the time it will be
      discarded or replaced.
2. Intangible assets include goodwill, patents, copyrights, and trademarks.
3. The difference between the two sides of an account is known as the balance.
   It may be either a debit balance or a credit balance. In the balance sheet the
   difference between the two sides is either . . . or . . .
4. Rückstellungen bildet ein Unternehmen zur Abdeckung von Verbindlichkeiten,
   die sich der Höhe nach nicht oder nicht genau bestimmen lassen.
5. Rücklagen sind eine Art Ersparnisse. Das Unternehmen bildet sie zur Deckung
   noch nicht entstandener Verbindlichkeiten. Man unterscheidet zwischen
   gesetzlichen und freien Rücklagen.
6. Die linke Seite einer Bilanz (Aktiva) zeigt, wie das Vermögen einer Firma
   angelegt ist, die rechte Seite (Passiva) läßt erkennen, woher die Gelder der
   Firma kommen. Wenn man von den Aktiva die Verbindlichkeiten absetzt, erhält
   man das Eigenkapital.
7. Die Gewinn- und Verlustrechnung weist den Reingewinn oder Reinverlust
   eines Zeitabschnittes, meist eines Geschäftsjahres, aus.
8. Der diesjährige Verlust erlaubt der Firma keine Zahlung einer Dividende für
   Stamm- und Vorzugsaktien.
9. Das Unternehmen hat sich der negativen wirtschaftlichen Entwicklung nicht
   entziehen können.
10. Das wirtschaftliche Eigenkapital – Nennkapital, Rücklagen und 50 Prozent des
    Sonderpostens mit Rücklageanteil – nahm um 580 Millionen DM ab.
11. Das Angebot von Aktien zum Vorzugspreis an Mitarbeiter gehört zu den
    freiwilligen sozialen Leistungen.

F. Please write a directors' report for each of the following two companies.

UNTERNEHMEN 1

Es handelt sich um ein Unternehmen der Maschinenbaubranche, das seit 1905
etabliert ist. Es ist sehr stark exportorientiert und verkauft viel in Europa. Durch

jahrzehntelange Erfolge (vor allem auf dem Exportmarkt) hat sich ein gutes finanzielles Polster gebildet. Jetzt, in der europaweiten Rezession, reduzieren sich die Gewinne. Eine Tochtergesellschaft wurde verkauft, eine Niederlassung im Ausland geschlossen. Mitarbeiter wurden entlassen, vor allem im Mittleren Management. Die Investitionen mußten verringert werden. Die Herstellungskosten müssen durch Rationalisierung herabgesetzt werden, um konkurrenzfähig zu bleiben. Die Weltkonjunktur insgesamt hat sich verschlechtert.

UNTERNEHMEN 2

Dies ist ein Unternehmen der Pharmaindustrie. Es wurde 1989 gegründet. Im letzten Jahr wurden neue Aktien ausgegeben, um das Eigenkapital aufzustocken. Das Personal wurde ebenfalls aufgestockt. Ein neues Vorstandsmitglied konnte gewonnen werden, mit viel Marketing-Erfahrung. Der Export, vor allem nach Amerika, konnte ausgeweitet werden. Die Forschungs- und Entwicklungskosten sind von Anfang her sehr hoch gewesen und sind jedes Jahr noch gestiegen. Insgesamt hat sich dieses Jahr ein Verlust wieder nicht vermeiden lassen. Aber die Tendenz ist sinkend. Ein neues Präparat steht kurz vor der Patentierung, für das die Firma keine Konkurrenz hat. Zuversicht auf Gewinn für nächstes Jahr.

Lösungen zu den Übungen
Answers to exercises

A.

1. Finanzanlagen
2. Bilanzgewinn
3. Gewinnrücklagen
4. immaterielle Vermögensgegenstände
5. gezeichnetes Kapital
6. nirgends
7. Forderungen und sonstige Vermögensgegenstände
8. Vorräte

B.

1. Steuern vom Einkommen und vom Ertrag
2. Umsatzerlöse
3. sonstige betriebliche Erträge
4. sonstige Steuern
5. Umsatzerlöse
6. Materialaufwand
7. sonstige betriebliche Aufwendungen
8. sonstige betriebliche Aufwendungen

C.

1. b
2. a
3. d
4. b und d

D.

1. siehe Kapitel 3, Seite 23 und Seite 26.
2. siehe Kapitel 3, Seite 22f.
3. Fremdkapital, weil Rückstellungen Verbindlichkeiten gegenüber Dritten sind.
4. siehe Kapitel 5, Seite 68.
5. siehe Kapitel 5, Seite 68.
6. Zusammenfassung der einzelnen Jahresabschlüsse von Konzernmitgliedern zu einem Konzernjahresabschluß.
7. siehe Kapitel 3, Seite 22.

E.

1. Zur Berechnung der Abschreibung braucht man
   a die ursprünglichen Kosten des Anlageguts
   b die voraussichtliche Nutzungsdauer der Anlage
   c den geschätzten Tausch- oder Schrottwert des Anlagegegenstands zum Zeitpunkt der Veräußerung.
2. Immaterielle Vermögensgegenstände umfassen Geschäftswert, Patente, Urheberrechte und Warenzeichen.
3. . . . balance sheet profit . . ., . . . balance sheet loss. . . . Der Unterschied zwischen den beiden Seiten eines Kontos wird Saldo genannt. Er kann entweder ein Sollsaldo oder ein Habensaldo sein. In der Bilanz heißt dieser Unterschied entweder Bilanzgewinn oder Bilanzverlust.
4. A business creates provisions to cover liabilities the amount of which cannot be determined exactly.
5. Reserves are a kind of savings. A business sets aside reserves in order to cover liabilities which have not yet arisen. One distinguishes between legal reserves and free reserves.
6. The left-hand side of the balance sheet (assets) shows how a business has applied its funds, the right-hand side (capital and liabilities) explains where the business funds come from. If you deduct provisions and creditors from the total assets you arrive at 'capital and reserves'.
7. The profit and loss account shows the net profit or net loss for a period of time, usually an accounting year.
8. The current year loss does not allow the company to pay a dividend on ordinary and preference shares.
9. The business has not been able to escape the negative economic development.
10. The shareholders' fund – share capital, reserves and 50 per cent of special tax-allowable reserve – decreased by 580 million DM.
11. The offer to buy shares at a reduced rate (share option) to employees is a voluntary social benefit.

7 Muster-Jahresabschlüsse

Specimen annual reports

Deutsche Lufthansa AG and **Lufthansa Konzern**
(*By kind permission of Lufthansa AG*)

Hoechst AG
(*By kind permission of Hoechst AG*)

Kaufhof Holding AG, Köln
(*By kind permission of Kaufhof Holding AG*)

Deutsche Lufthansa AG
Konzernbilanz zum 31. Dezember 1991

Aktiva	Anhang	TDM 31.12.1991	TDM 31.12.1991	TDM 31.12.1990
Immaterielle Vermögensgegenstände		290 275		298 359
Flugzeuge		9 227 184		8 397 706
Übrige Sachanlagen		1 473 347		1 418 878
Finanzanlagen	6)	789 839		716 035
Anlagevermögen	5)		**11 780 645**	**10 830 978**
Kapitalanlagen aus dem Versicherungsgeschäft			**83 049**	**78 356**
Vorräte	7)	1 344 427		1 067 616
Forderungen aus Lieferungen und Leistungen	8)	1 634 920		1 421 346
Übrige Forderungen und sonstige Vermögensgegenstände	8)	739 042		673 308
Wertpapiere	9)	1 016		4 767
Schecks, Kassenbestand, Bundesbank- und Postgiroguthaben, Guthaben bei Kreditinstituten	9)	305 764		407 075
Umlaufvermögen			**4 025 169**	**3 574 112**
Rechnungsabgrenzungsposten	10)		**65 318**	**56 183**
Bilanzsumme			**15 954 181**	**14 539 629**

Deutsche Lufthansa AG
Konzernbilanz zum 31. Dezember 1991

Passiva	Anhang	TDM 31.12.1991	TDM 31.12.1991	TDM 31.12.1990
Gezeichnetes Kapital	11)	1 526 000		1 526 000
Kapitalrücklage	12)	1 307 433		1 307 433
Gewinnrücklagen	12)	253 071		256 839
Konzernbilanzverlust/-gewinn		− 444 031		6 650
Anteile anderer Gesellschafter		44 285		47 162
Eigenkapital			**2 686 758**	**3 144 084**
Sonderposten mit Rücklageanteil	13)		**1 897 407**	**2 156 000**
Rückstellungen	14)		**3 433 305**	**2 991 706**
Anleihen		4 000 000		3 000 000
Verbindlichkeiten gegenüber Kreditinstituten		1 230 100		1 208 880
Übrige Verbindlichkeiten		2 695 930		2 028 542
Verbindlichkeiten	15)		**7 926 030**	**6 237 422**
Rechnungsabgrenzungsposten			**10 681**	**10 417**
Bilanzsumme			**15 954 181**	**14 539 629**

Deutsche Lufthansa AG
Bilanz zum 31. Dezember 1991

Aktiva	Anhang	TDM 31.12.1991	TDM 31.12.1991	TDM 31.12.1990
Immaterielle Vermögensgegenstände		260 468		284 131
Flugzeuge		8 160 657		7 828 706
Übrige Sachanlagen		1 225 113		1 195 650
Finanzanlagen	6)	819 054		730 451
Anlagevermögen	5)		**10 465 292**	**10 038 938**
Vorräte	7)	1 211 110		994 692
Forderungen aus Lieferungen und Leistungen	8)	1 559 233		1 198 585
Übrige Forderungen und sonstige Vermögensgegenstände	8)	760 872		574 359
Wertpapiere	9)	1 016		4 767
Schecks, Kassenbestand, Bundesbank- und Postgiroguthaben, Guthaben bei Kreditinstituten	9)	229 454		346 487
Umlaufvermögen			**3 761 685**	**3 118 890**
Rechnungsabgrenzungsposten	10)		**29 359**	**20 593**
Bilanzsumme			**14 256 336**	**13 178 421**

Deutsche Lufthansa AG
Bilanz zum 31. Dezember 1991

Passiva	Anhang	TDM 31.12.1991	TDM 31.12.1991	TDM 31.12.1990
Gezeichnetes Kapital	11)	1 526 000		1 526 000
Kapitalrücklage	12)	1 307 433		1 307 433
Gewinnrücklagen	12)	346 452		346 452
Bilanzverlust/-gewinn	32)	− 444 031		6 650
Eigenkapital			**2 735 854**	**3 186 535**
Sonderposten mit Rücklageanteil	13)		**1 856 213**	**2 113 626**
Rückstellungen	14)		**3 086 970**	**2 623 673**
Verbindlichkeiten gegenüber Kreditinstituten		450 285		527 685
Verbindlichkeiten gegenüber verbundenen Unternehmen		4 129 258		3 160 088
Übrige Verbindlichkeiten		1 996 735		1 564 991
Verbindlichkeiten	15)		**6 576 278**	**5 252 764**
Rechnungsabgrenzungsposten			**1 021**	**1 823**
Bilanzsumme			**14 256 336**	**13 178 421**

Deutsche Lufthansa AG
Konzern-Gewinn- und Verlustrechnung für das
Geschäftsjahr 1991

	Anhang	TDM 1991	TDM 1991	TDM 1990
Erlöse aus den Verkehrsleistungen	18)	14 266 140		12 694 805
Andere Betriebserlöse	19)	1 834 441		1 752 281
Umsatzerlöse		**16 100 581**		**14 447 086**
Bestandsveränderungen und andere aktivierte Eigenleistungen	20)	135 410		87 963
Sonstige betriebliche Erträge	21)	1 456 754		1 762 318
Materialaufwand	22)	− 6 965 519		− 6 239 854
Personalaufwand	23)	− 5 214 293		− 4 768 728
Abschreibungen	24)	− 1 513 521		− 1 327 028
Sonstige betriebliche Aufwendungen	25)	− 3 987 798		− 3 655 798
Ergebnis der betrieblichen Tätigkeit			**+ 11 614**	**+ 305 959**
Beteiligungsergebnis	26)	+ 51 625		+ 43 724
Zinsergebnis	27)	− 339 227		− 166 811
Abschreibungen auf Finanzanlagen und auf Wertpapiere des Umlaufvermögens		− 24 945		− 40 426
Finanzergebnis			**− 312 547**	**− 163 513**
Ergebnis der gewöhnlichen Geschäftstätigkeit	28)		**− 300 933**	**+ 142 446**
Steuern	29)		− 124 862	− 127 289
Jahresfehlbetrag/-überschuß			**− 425 795**	**+ 15 157**
Entnahmen aus Gewinnrücklagen			36 619	1 803
Einstellungen in Gewinnrücklagen			− 44 573	− 6 244
Anderen Gesellschaftern zustehender Verlust/Gewinn			− 10 282	− 4 066
Konzernbilanzverlust/-gewinn			**− 444 031**	**+ 6 650**

Deutsche Lufthansa AG
Gewinn- und Verlustrechnung für das Geschäftsjahr 1991

	Anhang	TDM 1991	TDM 1991	TDM 1990
Erlöse aus den Verkehrsleistungen	18)	12 885 523		11 501 734
Andere Betriebserlöse	19)	1 432 097		1 304 252
Umsatzerlöse		**14 317 620**		**12 805 986**
Bestandsveränderungen und andere aktivierte Eigenleistungen	20)	134 372		86 340
Sonstige betriebliche Erträge	21)	1 384 852		1 602 171
Materialaufwand	22)	− 6 433 662		− 5 646 386
Personalaufwand	23)	− 4 474 605		− 4 105 930
Abschreibungen	24)	− 1 366 029		− 1 215 883
Sonstige betriebliche Aufwendungen	25)	− 3 638 898		− 3 333 629
Ergebnis der betrieblichen Tätigkeit			**− 76 350**	**+ 192 669**
Beteiligungsergebnis	26)	+ 44 364		+ 96 992
Zinsergebnis	27)	− 293 216		− 159 530
Abschreibungen auf Finanzanlagen und auf Wertpapiere des Umlaufvermögens		− 5 761		− 3 342
Finanzergebnis			**− 254 613**	**− 65 880**
Ergebnis der gewöhnlichen Geschäftstätigkeit	28)		**− 330 963**	**+ 126 789**
Steuern	29)		− 113 068	− 118 123
Jahresfehlbetrag/-überschuß			**− 444 031**	**+ 8 666**
Einstellungen in andere Gewinnrücklagen			−	− 2 016
Bilanzverlust/-gewinn	32)		**− 444 031**	**+ 6 650**

Hoechst AG
Bilanz zum 31. Dezember 1990

Aktiva	Anhang*	31. 12.1990 Mio DM	31. 12. 1989 Mio DM
Immaterielle Vermögensgegenstände		54	38
Sachanlagen		4371	4238
Finanzanlagen		7241	6637
Anlagevermögen	(1)	**11666**	**10913**
Vorräte	(2)	**2093**	**2050**
Forderungen aus Lieferungen und Leistungen	(3) (5)	2472	2594
Andere Forderungen und sonstige Vermögensgegenstände	(4) (5)	1071	870
Forderungen und sonstige Vermögensgegenstände		**3543**	**3464**
Wertpapiere	(6)	747	1199
Schecks, Kassenbestand, Bundesbank- und Postgiroguthaben, Guthaben bei Kreditinstituten		383	420
Flüssige Mittel		**1130**	**1619**
Rechnungsabgrenzungsposten	(7)	·	·
Umlaufvermögen		**6766**	**7133**
		18432	18046

Passiva

Gezeichnetes Kapital	(9)	2902	2884
Kapitalrücklage		3853	3823
Gewinnrücklagen		2997	2847
Bilanzgewinn	(11)	755	750
Eigenkapital	(8)	**10507**	**10304**
Sonderposten mit Rücklageanteil	(12)	**974**	**1052**
Rückstellungen für Pensionen und ähnliche Verpflichtungen	(13)	2866	2741
Andere Rückstellungen	(14)	1665	1745
Rückstellungen		**4531**	**4486**
Finanzschulden	(15)	247	306
Verbindlichkeiten aus Lieferungen und Leistungen	(15)	872	795
Übrige Verbindlichkeiten	(15)	1301	1103
Verbindlichkeiten		**2420**	**2204**
Rechnungsabgrenzungsposten		·	·
		18432	18046

Hoechst AG
Gewinn- und Verlustrechnung zum 31. Dezember 1990

	Anhang*		1990 Mio DM *	1989 Mjo DM
Umsatzerlöse	(16)		**16 622**	**16 863**
Herstellungskosten der verkauften Leistungen		–	11 848	11 794
Bruttoergebnis vom Umsatz			**4 774**	**5 069**
Vertriebskosten		–	2 471	2 469
Forschungskosten		–	1 166	1 087
Allgemeine Verwaltungskosten		–	392	389
Sonstige betriebliche Erträge	(17)	+	320	333
Sonstige betriebliche Aufwendungen	(18)	–	159	220
Ergebnis aus Betriebstätigkeit			**906**	**1 237**
Beteiligungsergebnis	(19)	+	745	906
Zinserträge (Saldo)	(20)	+	86	127
Sonstige finanzielle Aufwendungen und Erträge	(21)	–	20	64
Ergebnis aus gewöhnlicher Geschäftstätigkeit/				
Gewinn vor Ertragsteuern			**1 717**	**2 206**
Steuern vom Einkommen und Ertrag	(22)	–	812	1 032
Jahresüberschuß			**905**	**1 174**

* siehe entsprechende Erläuterungen auf Seite 44 ff

Bestätigungsvermerk

Der Abschlußprüfer hat folgenden Bestätigungsvermerk erteilt:

Die Buchführung und der Jahresabschluß entsprechen nach unserer pflichtgemäßen Prüfung den gesetzlichen Vorschriften. Der Jahresabschluß vermittelt unter Beachtung der Grundsätze ordnungsmäßiger Buchführung ein den tatsächlichen Verhältnissen entsprechendes Bild der Vermögens-, Finanz- und Ertragslage der Hoechst AG. Der Anhang und der Lagebericht der Hoechst AG sind mit dem Konzernanhang und dem Konzernlagebericht zusammengefaßt worden. Der Lagebericht steht im Einklang mit dem Jahresabschluß.

Frankfurt am Main, den 25. März 1991

Treuhand-Vereinigung Aktiengesellschaft
Wirtschaftsprüfungsgesellschaft und Steuerberatungsgesellschaft

Dr. Kroneberger
Wirtschaftsprüfer

Seif
Wirtschaftsprüfer

Kaufhof Holding Aktiengesellschaft, Köln
Bilanz zum 31. Dezember 1992

Aktiva

	Anhang Ziffer	DM	DM	**Stand 31.12.1992 DM**	Stand 31.12.1991 TDM
A. Anlagevermögen	5				
I. Immaterielle Vermögensgegenstände					
Nutzungs- und andere Rechte			5.033.699		4.959
II. Sachanlagen	7				
1. Grundstücke, grundstücksgleiche Rechte und Bauten einschließlich der Bauten auf fremden Grundstücken und der Mietereinbauten		605.851.610			601.366
2. Andere Anlagen, Betriebs- und Geschäftsausstattung		13.936.286			18.116
3. Geleistete Anzahlungen und Anlagen im Bau		10.015.591			20.058
			629.803.487		639.540
III. Finanzanlagen	8				
1. Anteile an verbundenen Unternehmen		1.495.980.759			1.345.280
2. Ausleihungen an verbundene Unternehmen		16.375.000			16.750
3. Beteiligungen		175.708.075			35.554
4. Ausleihungen an Unternehmen, mit denen ein Beteiligungsverhältnis besteht		6.737.052			7.184
5. Sonstige Ausleihungen		1.047.118			1.271
6. Miet- und Pachtvorauszahlungen		10.956.442			11.432
			1.706.804.446		1.417.471
				2.341.641.632	2.061.970
B. Umlaufvermögen					
I. Forderungen und sonstige Vermögensgegenstände	9				
1. Forderungen aus Lieferungen und Leistungen		51.978			127
2. Forderungen gegen verbundene Unternehmen		738.061.659			926.852
3. Forderungen gegen Unternehmen, mit denen ein Beteiligungsverhältnis besteht		5.911.888			10.418
4. Sonstige Vermögensgegenstände		48.161.262			46.193
			792.186.787		983.590
II. Wertpapiere					
Sonstige Wertpapiere			21.887.829		18.784
III. Schecks, Kassenbestand, Guthaben bei Kreditinstituten			2.223.657		11.446
				816.298.273	1.013.820
C. Rechnungsabgrenzungsposten				**18.214.445**	18.371
				3.176.154.350	3.094.161

Kaufhof Holding Aktiengesellschaft, Köln
Bilanz zum 31. Dezember 1992

Passiva

	Anhang Ziffer	DM	DM	DM	**Stand 31.12.1992 DM**	Stand 31.12.1991 TDM
A. Eigenkapital						
I. Gezeichnetes Kapital	11			448.635.150		446.493
(Bedingtes Kapital: 130.126.500 DM)						
II. Kapitalrücklage	12					
Vortrag 1.1.1992			871.333.661			
Einstellung			7.582.680	878.916.341		871.334
III. Gewinnrücklagen						
1. Gesetzliche Rücklage			47.375.447			47.375
2. Andere Gewinnrücklagen	13					
Vortrag 1.1.1992		481.759.747				
Einstellung aus dem Jahresüberschuß		33.497.000	515.256.747			481.760
				562.632.194		529.135
IV. Bilanzgewinn				109.258.869		108.745
					1.999.442.554	1.955.707
B. Sonderposten mit Rücklageanteil						
1. Rücklage gemäß § 6 b EStG				24.142.987		29.273
2. Rücklage gemäß § 52 Abs. 8 EStG				402.823		805
					24.545.810	30.078
C. Rückstellungen						
1. Rückstellungen für Pensionen und ähnliche Verpflichtungen				106.020.099		104.105
2. Steuerrückstellungen				43.113.042		40.385
3. Sonstige Rückstellungen	17			70.107.789		76.253
					219.240.930	220.743
D. Verbindlichkeiten	18					
1. Anleihen				85.000.000		–
2. Verbindlichkeiten gegenüber Kreditinstituten				18.035.029		11.912
3. Verbindlichkeiten aus Lieferungen und Leistungen				46.899.591		32.466
4. Verbindlichkeiten gegenüber verbundenen Unternehmen				551.910.442		676.702
5. Verbindlichkeiten gegenüber Unternehmen, mit denen ein Beteiligungsverhältnis besteht				303.111		134
6. Sonstige Verbindlichkeiten				230.722.562		162.571
					932.870.735	883.785
E. Rechnungsabgrenzungsposten					**54.321**	3.848
					3.176.154.350	3.094.161

Kaufhof Holding Aktiengesellschaft, Köln
Gewinn- und Verlustrechnung für das Geschäftsjahr 1992

	Anhang Ziffer	1992 DM	1992 DM	1991 TDM	1991 TDM
1. Umsatzerlöse (brutto)		291.938.609		293.786	
2. Umsatzsteuer		1.777.447		1.674	
3. Umsatzerlöse (netto)			290.161.162		292.112.
4. Andere aktivierte Eigenleistungen			–		600
5. Sonstige betriebliche Erträge	22		238.857.942		241.376
6. Materialaufwand: Aufwendungen für bezogene Leistungen			144.507.973		135.681
7. Personalaufwand: a) Gehälter und Löhne		82.197.700		81.178	
b) Soziale Abgaben und Aufwendungen für Altersversorgung und für Unterstützung (davon für Altersversorgung: 16.651.477 DM)		27.220.071	109.417.771	32.119	113.297
8. Abschreibungen auf immaterielle Vermögensgegenstände des Anlagevermögens und Sachanlagen	25		92.892.783		76.452
9. Sonstige betriebliche Aufwendungen	26		193.355.752		184.167
10. Erträge aus Gewinnabführungsverträgen			101.106.284		119.382
11. Erträge aus Beteiligungen (davon aus verbundenen Unternehmen: 143.853.601 DM)			149.114.372		126.533
12. Erträge aus Ausleihungen des Finanzanlagevermögens (davon aus verbundenen Unternehmen: 1.605.919 DM)			2.432.642		2.766
13. Sonstige Zinsen und ähnliche Erträge (davon aus verbundenen Unternehmen: 115.063.569 DM)			198.109.178		132.917
14. Abschreibungen auf Finanzanlagen und auf Wertpapiere des Umlaufvermögens			616.435		277
15. Zinsen und ähnliche Aufwendungen (davon an verbundene Unternehmen: 38.669.544 DM)			194.871.525		137.016
16. Aufwendungen aus Verlustübernahmen			17.608.894		514
17. **Ergebnis der gewöhnlichen Geschäftstätigkeit**			226.510.447		268.282
18. Außerordentliche Erträge		–		50.834	
19. Außerordentliche Aufwendungen		–		108.439	
20. Außerordentliches Ergebnis			–		57.605
21. Steuern vom Einkommen und vom Ertrag davon an Organgesellschaften weiterbelastet	29	93.623.894 24.343.849	69.280.045	104.070 31.014	73.056
22. Sonstige Steuern davon an Organgesellschaften weiterbelastet	29	19.759.333 5.284.800	14.474.533	18.103 4.953	13.150
23. **Jahresüberschuß**	30		142.755.869		124.471
24. Einstellung aus dem Jahresüberschuß in andere Gewinnrücklagen			33.497.000		15.726
25. **Bilanzgewinn**	34		109.258.869		108.745

8 Glossar

Glossary

Please note that both sections of this glossary contain terminology and explanations as they apply in the context of accounting. Possible other meanings have not been included.

Deutsch—Englisch

A

Abgänge (*pl*) disposals, leavers (of employees)

abgerechnete Leistungen invoiced (sales of) services

Abgrenzung, die (-en) accrual or deferral

abrechnen to invoice (goods and services), to settle (an account), to charge (an account), to clear (a cheque)

Abrechnungszeitraum, der (-äume) accounting period/financial period

Abschluß, der (-üsse) accounts/financial statements

Abschlußprüfer, der (-) auditor

Abschlußprüfung, die (-en) audit

Abschreibung, die (-en) depreciation (tangible assets)/amortisation (intangible assets), amounts written off (investments)

Abschreibungen auf Finanzanlagen und auf Wertpapiere des Umlauf-vermögens amounts written off fixed-asset investments (= long-term) and current-asset investments (= short-term) [write-down of financial assets and short-term investments]

Abschreibungen auf immaterielle Vermögensgegenstände amortisation of intangible (fixed) assets

Abschreibungen auf immaterielle Vermögensgegenstände des Anlagevermögens und Sachanlagen amortisation of intangible and depreciation of tangible fixed assets

Abschreibungen auf Sachanlagen depreciation of tangible fixed assets

Abschreibungsmethode, die (-en) depreciation method

Abschreibungssatz, der (-ätze) depreciation rate

absetzen (*sep*) to deduct/to subtract

Agio, das 1. premium 2. share premium (= difference between the nominal value of a share and its market value e.g. 10p shares traded at £2.10 have a nominal value of 10p and a share premium of £2)

Aktie, die (-n) share (AG)

Aktienemission, die (-en) issue of shares

Aktionär, der (-e) shareholder (AG)

Aktiva (*pl*) assets (= all items on the left-hand side of a German balance sheet)

aktive Rechnungsabgrenzungsposten (*pl*) prepayments and accrued income

aktivieren to capitalise [to capitalize] (= to recognise/carry as an asset)

aktivierte Aufwendungen capitalised costs

aktivierte Aufwendungen für die Ingangsetzung und Erweiterung des Geschäftsbetriebs start-up and business expansion costs capitalised

aktivierte Eigenleistungen own work capitalised [capitalized in-house output] (= internally produced and capitalised assets)

aktivisch on the asset side

Altersversorgung, die old-age social security system/pension provisions

andere aktivierte Eigenleistungen own work capitalised* [other capitalised in-house output] (= other internally produced and capitalised assets)

andere Anlagen other plant

andere Erlöse sundry sales

andere Gewinnrücklagen other revenue reserves

anfallen (*sep*) to fall due/arise/accrue (costs), to accumulate (interest)

Anhang, der notes to the financial statements

Anlage, die (-n) 1. plant 2. investment

Anlagegut, das (-üter) tangible fixed asset

Anlagen im Bau assets in the course of construction

Anlagenbau, der plant building in progress

Anlagenspiegel, der (-) fixed asset movement schedule/fixed asset schedule

Anlagevermögen, das (-) fixed assets*

Anleger, der (-) investor

Anleihe, die (-n) loan, debenture, bond

Anleihen, davon konvertibel debenture loans/loans, of which convertible

Anschaffungskosten (*pl*) purchase price(s)/acquisition cost(s)

ansetzen (*sep*) to determine/to fix

Anteil, der share

Anteile (*pl*) shares/interests/ participations (in companies, partnerships or other forms of association)

Anteile an assoziierten Unternehmen shares in associated undertakings [enterprises]

Anteile an verbundenen Unternehmen shares in group undertakings [shares in affiliated enterprises]

Anteile anderer Gesellschafter minority interests* (= minority shareholders' part in the consolidated 'capital and reserves')

Anteile im Fremdbesitz minority interests* (= minority shareholders' part in the consolidated 'capital and reserves')

Anteile Konzernfremder am Jahresergebnis minority interest in the profit or loss for the current year (= minority shareholders' part in the consolidated profit or loss)

Anteilseigner, der (-) shareholder [stockholder, equity holder], shareholder in a GmbH

anzahlen to make a down payment/to make an advance payment/to pay a deposit

Anzahlung, die (-en) down payment/advance payment/deposit

Arbeitgeber, der (-) employer

Arbeitnehmer, der (-) employee

Arbeitslosenversicherung, die unemployment insurance

assoziiertes Unternehmen associated undertaking

Aufgeld, das, see Agio

auditieren to audit (the books of accounts)

auf konzernfremde Gesellschafter entfallender Verlust loss attributable to minority interests (i.e. minority interest shareholders)

Auflistung, die (-en) listing

Auflösung von Rückstellungen reversal [writing back] of provisions (= previously expected charges did not occur and are therefore cancelled)

Auflösung von Steuerrückstellungen reversal [writing back] of tax provisions (previously expected tax charges did not arise and are therefore cancelled)

aufnehmen (*sep*) to take out (a loan), to raise (capital)

aufrechnen (*sep*) (*gegeneinander*) to net off

aufstellen (*sep*) to set up/to draw up/to prepare (the annual report)

Aufwärtsentwicklung, die upward trend

Aufwendungen (*pl*) charges/costs/expenditure

Aufwendungen für Altersversorgung pension costs

Aufwendungen für bezogene Leistungen cost of purchased/bought-in services

Aufwendungen für bezogene Waren cost of purchased/bought-in goods

Aufwendungen für Roh-, Hilfs- und Betriebsstoffe cost of raw materials and consumables*

Aufwendungen für Schließungen closure costs

Aufwendungen für Unterstützung other social costs

Aufwendungen aus Verlustübernahmen loss transfers

Aufwendungen für vorzeitige Pensionierung und Sozialplan charges for early retirement and social fund for employees

ausbuchen to take out of the books, to write off

ausschütten to distribute (profits), to pay dividends

außerordentliche Aufwendungen extraordinary charges*

außerordentliche Erträge extraordinary income*

außerordentliches Ergebnis extraordinary profit or loss*/extraordinary result

außerplanmßig unscheduled/exceptional

außerplanmäßige Abschreibungen exceptional depreciation charges (= in excess of the normal depreciation charges)

Ausfuhr, die export/exports

Ausfuhrzoll, der (-ölle) customs duty on exports

Ausgaben (*pl*) expenditure

ausgebuchte Forderungen debtors written off/bad debts written off

Auslandsmarkt, der (-ärkte) foreign market

Ausleihung, die (-en) loan

Ausleihungen an Unternehmen, mit denen ein Beteiligungsverhältnis besteht loans to undertakings in which the company has a participating interest [loans to enterprises in which participations are held]

Ausleihungen an verbundene Unternehmen loans to group undertakings (=subsidiaries) [loans to affiliated enterprises]

Ausleihungen des Finanzanlagevermögens long-term loans

Ausschüttung, die (-en) dividend payment/distribution (of profits)

ausstehend owing/outstanding

ausstehende Rechnung accrual (= outstanding payment)

B

Bankdarlehen, das (-) bank loan

Bankguthaben, das (-) cash at bank, credit-balance in bank account

Bankspesen (pl) bank charges, bank fees

Bargeld, das cash

Bau, der construction, building

Baubranche, die construction (industry)

Bauten (pl) buildings

Bauten auf fremden Grundstücken buildings on third-party land

bedingtes Kapital conditional capital (= additional share capital authorised for future issue conditional on conversion rights or share options being exercised)

Beitrag, der (-äge) contribution

Beiträge an Berufsvertretungen contributions to professional bodies and associations

Beitragssatz, der (-ätze) rate of contribution

belaufen auf (refl) to amount to

belegen mit to allocate, to use

Berichtigung, die (-en) correction/adjustment

Berichtsjahr, das (-e) accounting year/financial year

Berufsgenossenschaftsbeitrag, der (-äge) contribution for occupational accident insurance

Berufsvertretung, die (-en) professional body or association

Bestand, der stock(s) [inventory(-ies)]

Bestände (pl) stock(s) [inventory(-ies)]

Beständerechnung, die (-en) calculation of stock [inventory], statement of stocks [inventories]

Bestandsaufnahme, die (-n) stocktaking [inventory taking]

Bestandsveränderungen (pl) stock [inventory] changes/change in stocks of finished goods and in work-in-progress* [change in finished inventories and in work-in-process]

Bestätigungsvermerk, der audit opinion/audit report

Bestellung, die (-en) order (e.g. customer/sales order, purchase order)

beteiligt sein to participate

Beteiligung, die (-en) share holding/stake/investment, participating interest [participation] (= term used for all interests in other German businesses of more than 20% of shares and/or voting rights; where certain interests are stated separately e.g. verbundene Unternehmen (subsidiaries), only the remaining interests are represented in this term)

Beteiligungsaufwendungen (pl) charges related to investment in shares

Beteiligungsergebnis, das net income from investments in other undertakings (= comprises net income from participating interests, associated undertakings, subsidiary undertakings etc.)

Beteiligungsverhältnis, das (-se) percentage of participation (= relationship of participation)

Betrieb, der plant, operation

betriebliche Erträge operating income [operating revenue]

Betriebsaufwendungen (pl) operating charges

Betriebsausstattung, die (-en) fixtures and fittings of a plant

Betriebserlöse (pl) operating income [operating revenue]

betriebsfremdes Ergebnis profit or loss/result from non-operating activities (= usually investment activities)

betriebsgewöhnliche Nutzungsdauer normal period of business use (of assets)

Betriebskrankenkasse, die (-n) company health insurance fund

Betriebsstoffe (*pl*) consumables [supplies] (= not incorporated in manufactured item, e.g. grease for machines, repair materials)

bewegliche Sachanlagen (*pl*) movable tangible assets

Bewertungsgrundsatz, der (-ätze) accounting policy, method of valuation

bezogene Leistungen purchased/bought-in services

bezogene Waren purchased/bought-in goods

Bilanz, die (-en) balance sheet

Bilanzgewinn, der balance sheet profit (= current year profit adjusted for the balance sheet)

bilanzieren to prepare a balance sheet/to report in the balance sheet, to balance (an account)

Bilanzierungsgrundsatz, der (-ätze) accounting policy, basic principle of accounting

Bilanzierungs- und Bewertungsgrundsätze (*pl*) accounting policies

Bildung von Rückstellungen setting-up of provisions

Bonus, der (-ni) bonus

Börse, die (-n) stock exchange

Branche, die (-n) sector of industry, line of business, trade

Briefkurs, der selling rate of currencies

buchen to make an entry in the accounts/to post (to an account)

buchen, zu Lasten (*gen*) to debit (= to enter on the debit/left side of an account)

Buchwert, der (-e) (net) book value/carrying value (= original cost less accumulated depreciation)

Bundesbank, die German central bank

Bundesbankguthaben, das (-) central bank (credit) balance/central bank deposit

Bürgschaft, die (-en) guarantee [guaranty]

Bürobedarf, der stationery, office supplies

brutto gross (= before deductions)

Bruttoergebnis, das (-se) gross result/result before tax

Bruttoergebnis vom Umsatz turnover before tax

D

Darlehen, das (-) bank loan

Deckungsbetrag, der (-äge) amount of coverage

degressive Abschreibung reducing-balance depreciation

Dienstleistung, die (-en) service

Disagio, das discount, capitalised discount on interest-bearing investments (= difference between the amount received as loan e.g. 900DM, and the amount to be repaid at repayment date, e.g. 1000DM)

Dividende, die (-, -n) dividend

drohende Verluste aus schwebenden Geschäften probable losses from contractual commitments

durchführen (*sep*) to carry out, to implement

Durchschnittskurs, der (-e) average exchange rate

E

eigene Aktie own (AG) share (i.e. a public company itself – as a legal entity – has purchased its own shares)

eigener Anteil own (GmbH) share (i.e. a private company itself – as a legal entity – has purchased its own shares)

Eigenkapital, das (share) capital and reserves/shareholders' fund [shareholders' equity/equity]

Eigenkapitalquote, die (-n) percentage/proportion of capital (compared to liabilities)

Eigenleistung, die (-en) output of goods and services for own purposes

Einkaufskontrakt, der (-e) purchase contract

Einkommen, das (-) income/earnings

Einkommensquelle, die (-n) source of income

Einstandswert, der input value (= original cost of purchase/ manufacture)

Einstellung, die (-en) transfer/allocation to (a special reserve), discontinuance/closure

Einstellung in Sonderposten mit Rücklageanteil transfer to special tax-allowable reserve

Einstellung in Gewinnrücklagen
transfer to revenue reserves
enthalten to contain
Entnahmen aus Gewinnrücklagen
transfers from revenue reserves
entnehmen to transfer from (reserves), to withdraw
Erfolgsrechnung, die (-en) profit and loss account [income statement/statement of earnings]
Ergebnis, das (-se) result/profit or loss
Ergebnis aus assoziierten Unternehmen result (= net total of profit and loss transfers) from interests in associated undertakings
Ergebnis aus Betriebstätigkiet operating result/operating profit or loss
Ergebnis der betrieblichen Tätigkeit operating result/operating profit or loss
Ergebnis der gewöhnlichen Geschäftstätigkeit profit or loss on ordinary activities
erhaltene Anzahlungen auf Bestellungen payments received on account of customer orders
Erhöhung, die (-en) increase
Erhöhungen des Bestands an fertigen und unfertigen Erzeugnissen increase in stocks of finished goods and in work-in-progress [increase in finished inventories and in work-in-process]
Erhöhung des Bestands an unverrechneten Lieferungen und Leistungen increase in goods and services provided but not balanced off
Erläuterungen (*pl*) explanations
Erlös, der (-e) revenue/proceeds
Erlöse aus Nebengeschäften income from ancillary/minor business activities
ermitteln to determine, to calculate, to compute (tax)
Erstattung, die (-en) refund/repayment, tax refund
Erstattungen für Vorjahre tax refunds for previous years
Ertrag, der income/revenue/proceeds [earnings]
Erträge (*pl*) income
Erträge aus der Auflösung von Sonderposten mit Rücklageanteil income from the reversal [writing back]
of previous transfers to special tax-allowable reserve
Erträge aus Dienstleistungen income from services
Erträge aus Lizenzen income from licences
Erträge aus Gewinnübernahmen income from profit transfers
Erträge aus anderen Wertpapieren und Ausleihungen des Finanzanlagevermögens income from other investments and long-term loans
Erträge aus Beteiligungen income from participating interests (= dividends and similar income)
Erträge aus Beteiligungen an verbundenen Unternehmen income from shares in group undertakings [affiliated enterprises]
Erträge aus dem Abgang von Gegenständen des Anlagevermögens profit on the disposal of (any type of) fixed assets
Erträge aus dem Abgang von Gegenständen des Sachanlagevermögens profit on the disposal of tangible fixed assets
Erträge aus der Auflösung von Rückstellungen income from the reversal [writing back] of provisions
Erträge aus der Auflösung von Rückstellungen für sonstige Steuern income from the reversal [writing back] of provisions for other taxes
Erträge aus der Herabsetzung von Forderungswertberichtigungen und dem Eingang ausgebuchter Forderungen income from the reduction in doubtful debt provision and from the recovery [writing back] of bad debts previously written off
Erträge aus Gewinnabführverträgen income from profit transfer contracts
Ertragsbesteuerung, die the imposition of tax on profits
Ertragslage, die profit level
Ertragsteuer, die all taxes on profit [income] (= corporation tax, local government tax on profits, tax on investment income)

Ertragsteueraufwand, der cost of all taxes on profit [income] (= corporation tax, local government tax on profits, tax on investment income)

Erweiterung, die (-en) expansion

erwerben to acquire

Erzeugnis, das (-se) manufactured item/good/product

Eventualverbindlichkeit, die (-en) contingency/contingent liability

F

fertige Erzeugnisse finished goods

Fertigungslohn, der (-öhne) wages in manufacture

Fertigungsmaterial, das (-ien) production material

festverzinslich fixed-interest bearing

festverzinsliches Wertpapier fixed-interest bearing investment

Filiale, die (-n) branch

Finanzamt, das (-ämter) Inland Revenue

Finanzanlage, die (-n) long-term investment [financial asset]

Finanzbehörde, die (-n) Inland Revenue

Finanzergebnis, das profit or loss/result from non-operating activities (= usually investment activities)

Finanzierung, die financing/provision of funds

Finanzlage, die financial position

Firmenwert, der (-e) goodwill (= worth of a business over and above its actual assets)

flüssige Mittel (*pl*) liquid funds, cash at bank and in hand*

Forderung, die (-en) debtor [account receivable, receivable], trade debtor, customer account

Forderungen aus dem Versicherungsgeschäft debtors [receivables] from the insurance business

Forderungen aus Lieferungen und Leistungen debtors [receivables] for goods delivered and services rendered/trade debtors

Forderungen gegen Unternehmen, mit denen ein Beteiligungsverhältnis besteht amounts owed by undertakings in which the company has a participating interest* [receivables from enterprises in which participations are held]

Forderungen gegen verbundene Unternehmen amounts owed by group undertakings* [receivables from affiliated enterprises]

Forderungen und sonstige Vermögensgegenstände debtors [receivables] and other current assets

Forderungsausfall, der (-älle) bad debt [loss of receivable outstanding]

Forderungswertberichtigung, die (-en) doubtful debt provision

Format, das (-e) format

Forschung und Entwicklung research and development

freiwillige soziale Aufwendungen voluntary expenditure for staff (fringe benefits)

Fremdkapital, das liabilities/creditors and provisions for liabilities and charges

Fremdwährung, die (-en) foreign currency

Fremdwährungskursgewinne (*pl*) exchange rate gains on foreign currencies

G

Garantieverpflichtung, die (-en) guarantee [guaranty] obligation

Gegenstände des Anlagevermögens fixed asset items

Gegenstände des Sachanlagevermögens items from tangible fixed assets

Gegenstände des Umlaufvermögens current asset items

Gehalt, das (-älter) salary

Geldbestände (*pl*) cash in hand/petty cash

Geldkurs, der buying rate of currencies

Geldmittel (*pl*) cash resources/funds

geleistete Anzahlungen payments on account* [prepaid expenses]/advance payments to suppliers (of stocks or assets)

Gemeinkosten (*pl*) overhead costs/overheads

genehmigtes Kapital authorised capital (= additional share capital authorised for future issue)

Geschäftsablauf, der (-äufe) the course of business

Geschäftsanteil, der (-e) share/shareholding/interest/participation (GmbH)

Geschäftsausstattung, die (office) fixtures and fittings

Geschäftsbetrieb, der (-e) business/business establishment/(sum total of) business activities

Geschäftsführer, der (-) manager/chief executive/director

Geschäftsverlauf, der business activity

Geschäftsvorfall, der (-älle) business transaction

Geschäftswert, der (-e) goodwill* (= worth of a business over and above its actual assets)

Gesellschafter, der (-) shareholder/company member [stockholder] (in a GmbH), partner (in a partnership)

Gesellschaftsform, die (-en) legal form of a business (e.g. AG, GmbH, etc.)

gesetzliche Rücklage legal reserve (= reserve required by law, AktG)

Gewerbe, das (-) 1. business 2. trade 3. industry

Gewerbeertragsteuer, die tax on profits levied by local government (= similar to UK council taxes)

Gewerbekapitalsteuer, die tax on assets levied by local government (= similar to UK council taxes)

gewerblich commercial, industrial

gewerbliche Schutzrechte industrial property rights (e.g. patents, design patents, trademarks)

Gewinn, der (-e) profit/gain/earnings/net income

Gewinnabführvertrag, der (-äge) profit transfer contract

Gewinnausschüttung, die (-en) distribution of profits/dividend payout

Gewinne aus dem Verkauf von Beteiligungen profit on the sale of shares

Gewinne aus dem Verkauf von Sachanlagen profit on the sale of tangible fixed assets

Gewinnermittlung, die calculation/determination of profit

Gewinnrückgang, der drop in profits

Gewinnrücklage, die (-n) revenue reserve (= accumulated retained profits)

Gewinn- und Verlustrechnung, die profit and loss account [income statement/statement of earnings]

Gewinnvortrag, der (-äge) profit carried/brought forward (= previous years' profits accumulated)

gezeichnetes Kapital nominal capital, share capital [subscribed capital] (= capital with limited liability)

gezogener Wechsel draft (= bill of exchange issued but not yet accepted)

Girokonto, das (-ten) current account (at a bank)

Gläubiger, der (-) creditor

Grundkapital, das share capital (in AG)

Grundpfandrecht, das (e) right over land due to mortgage

Grundsätze ordnungsmäßiger Buchführung (GoB) Generally Accepted Accounting Principles (GAAP)

Grundsteuer, die tax on land levied by local government (= similar to UK council taxes)

Grundstück, das (-e) (plot of) land/real estate/real property/landholding (= freehold land)

grundstücksgleiche Bauten leasehold property/properties

grundstücksgleiche Rechte leasehold rights

Gut, das commodity

gutbringen (*sep*) to credit (= to enter on the credit/right side of an account)

gutschreiben (*sep*) to credit (= to enter on the credit/right side of an account)

Güter (*pl*) goods, commodities [merchandise]

Guthaben, das (-) credit balance/deposit

H

Haftung, die legal liability

halbfertig semi-finished

halbfertige Erzeugnisse work-in-progress* [work-in-process], semi-finished goods

Handel, der trade, commerce

Handelsbilanz, die (-en) commercial balance sheet

Handelsfirma, die (-en) trading business

handelsrechtlich as per commercial law
Hersteller, der (-) manufacturer/producer
Herstellungskosten (*pl*) cost of production/ manufacturing cost(s)/cost of sales
Herstellungspreis, der (-e) cost price
Hilfsstoffe (*pl*) consumables [supplies] (= auxiliary material incorporated in manufactured item, e.g. glue, paint)

I

im Rahmen der sozialen Sicherheit
within the framework of social security
im/in Bau under construction
immaterielle Vermögensgegenstände
intangible assets*
Industrie, die (-en) industry
Industrieland, das (-änder) industrialised country
Ingangsetzung, die start-up of a business
Inhaber, der (-) owner
Inhaberaktie, die (-n) bearer share (= share in bearer form is owned by the person in whose possession the share certificate is; it is freely transferable, e.g. ordinary and preference share in AG – rare in UK)
Innenumsatzerlöse (*pl*) internal turnover/sales (e.g. within a group, between branches)
insgesamt total
Instandhaltung, die repair and maintenance/upkeep

J

Jahresabschluß, der (-üsse) annual report/annual financial statements/annual accounts
Jahresabschlußkosten (*pl*) annual report preparation costs
Jahresergebnis, das (-sse) profit or loss for the year
Jahresfehlbetrag, der loss for the financial year [net loss for the year]
Jahresüberschuß, der profit for the financial year/annual net profit [net income for the year]
Jubiläumszuwendung, die (-en) anniversary gift/award to employees
juristische Person, die legal person/legal entity

K

Kalkulationsbasis, die basis of calculation
Kapital, das 1. share capital and reserves and liabilities (= all financial resources of a business) *Note*: in English the accountancy term capital does not refer to liabilities) 2. total assets of a business 3. investment (=money invested so as to produce a return, e.g. savings at bank, machinery, shares)
Kapitalanlage, die (-n) financial investment/investment
Kapitalanteil, der (-e) share in the capital (of a business)
Kapitalertragsteuer, die tax on investment income [Capital yields tax] (= tax on dividends, interest, etc.)
Kapitalgesellschaft, die (-en) incorporated business, company [corporation] (= type of business organisation with limited liability, i.e. company itself is a legal person)
Kapitalrücklage, die (-n) capital reserve/share premium account (= accumulated share premiums)
Kapitalseite, die (-n) capital and liabilities side
Kassenbestand, der (-ände) cash in the till, cash in hand, petty cash
Konjunkturschwäche, die weakness in the economy
Konkurs, der (-e) bankruptcy, compulsory winding up
konsolidieren to consolidate (= to combine the financial statements of several businesses into one set of accounts)
Konsolidierungskreis, der group of undertakings
konvertibel convertible
Konzern, der (-e) group (of undertakings)
Konzernbilanzgewinn, der (-e) balance sheet profit of group
Konzernbilanzverlust, der (-e) balance sheet loss of group
konzernfremden Gesellschaftern zustehender Gewinn profit attributable to minority interests (i.e. minority interest shareholders)
konzernfremder Gesellschafter
minority interest shareholder

Konzerngewinn, der (-e) group profit [consolidated retained earnings]

konzernintern within a group

Konzernmitglied, das (-er) member of a group (of undertakings)

Konzession, die (-en) concession, licence [license], franchise

Körperschaftsteuer, die corporation tax [corporation income tax/corporate tax] (= tax on business profits)

Kostendruck, der pressure on (e.g. manufacturing) costs

Kraftfahrzeugsteuer, die road tax

Kreditinstitut, das (-e) bank

kumuliert accumulated

kumulierte Abschreibungen accumulated depreciation/amortisation (= total of depreciation/amortisation charged so far)

Kunde, der (-n) customer/client, debtor [receivable]

Kundenstamm, der regular customers/established clientele

Kurs, der (-e) rate, exchange rate, market price

Kursgewinn, der (-e) exchange rate gain/exchange profit

L

Lagebericht, der (-e) directors' report [corporate management report]

Lagerbestand, der (-ände) goods in stock at warehouse, stock [inventory] level

latente Steuern deferred tax

Laufzeit, die (-en) term, life, time to maturity

Leasing, das leasing (provides long-term use of an asset without legal ownership)

Leasingverpflichtungen (*pl*) leasing obligations

Leistungen (*pl*) services

Lieferantenkredit, der (-e) trade credit

Lieferung, die (-en) delivery, supply

lineare Abschreibung straight-line depreciation

liquidieren to wind up/to liquidate

Lizenz, die (-en) permit, licence [license]

Lizenzerträge (*pl*) income from licences

Lohn, der (-öhne) wage(s)/pay

Löhne und Gehälter wages and salaries*

M

Marke, die (-n) brand (foods), make (industrial goods, e.g. car)

Markenartikel, der (-) brand product/article

Marktanteil, der (-e) market share

Materialaufwand, der (-ände) cost of materials

Miete, die (-en) rent

Mieteinnahmen (*pl*) rental income

Mietobjekt, das (-e) rented property

Mietverpflichtungen (*pl*) rent obligations

Mietvorauszahlung, die (-en) rent prepayment

Mineralölsteuer, die mineral oil tax

mit einer Restlaufzeit bis zu einem Jahr (amounts) falling due within one year

mit einer Restlaufzeit über fünf Jahre (amounts) falling due after more than five years

mit einer Restlaufzeit von mehr als einem Jahr (amounts) falling due after more than one year

Mitarbeiter, der (-) employee, co-worker

Mittelherkunft, die source of funds

Mittelkurs, der (-e) middle exchange rate (daily)

Muttergesellschaft, die (-en) parent company, parent undertaking

N

Nebengeschäft, das (-e) ancillary part of a business/secondary business activity

Nebenprodukt, das (-e) by-product

nicht abgerechnete Leistungen services provided but not invoiced

Nominalwert, der (-e) nominal value/par value (e.g. £2 shares have a nominal value of £2)

Nutzungsdauer, die period of use

O

Organgesellschaft, die (-en) dependent undertaking [dependent enterprise] (= fully owned or fully controlled subsidiary undertaking)

P

Pacht, die lease

Pachtvorauszahlung, die (-en) lease prepayment (on land or buildings)

Passiva (*pl*) capital and liabilities [liabilities and shareholders' equity] (= all items on the right-hand side of a German balance sheet)

passive Rechnungsabgrenzungsposten (*pl*) accruals and deferred income

passivisch on the capital and liabilities side

Patent, das (-e) patent

Patentierung, die (-en) issue of a patent

pauschal overall, average

Pauschalwertberichtigung, die overall depreciation, average depreciation

Pension, die (-en) retirement pension/employee pension/retirement benefit

Pensionierung, die (-en) retirement

Personalaufwand, der staff costs*/personnel costs/employment costs/payroll costs

Personalkosten (*pl*) staff costs/personnel costs/employment costs/payroll costs

Personalnebenkosten (*pl*) personnel/staff costs additional to employee remuneration (= employer's contributions and voluntary social costs, e.g. training courses)

Pflichtangaben (*pl*) compulsory details/information

planmäßige Abschreibungen normal/scheduled depreciation

Porto postage

Posten, der (-) entry/item (e.g. in balance sheet or profit and loss account)

Postgiroguthaben, das (-) postal giro (credit) balance/postal giro deposit

Prioritätsaktie, die (-en) preference share [preferred stock]

produzierendes Gewerbe manufacturing business

Provision, die (-en) commission

Prozeßrückstellungen (*pl*) provisions for litigation costs [provisions for expenses of lawsuit]

prüfen to audit (the accounts)

R

Rabatt, der (-e) rebate

Rationalisierungsmaßnahme, die (-n) rationalisation measure

real in real (= money) terms/net

Reallasten (*pl*) mortgages

Rechnung, die (-en) sales invoice/invoice [bill]

Rechnungsabgrenzungsposten, der (-) (*auf der Aktivseite*) prepayment or accrued income (= payment made in advance or income due but not yet received)

Rechnungsabgrenzungsposten, der- (*auf der Passivseite*) accrual or deferred income (= outstanding payment or income received but relating to future accounting period)

Rechnungsgrundsätze (*pl*) accounting principles

Rechnungsjahr, das (-e) financial year/accounting year

Rechnungslegung, die preparing and publishing of the annual report

Rechnungswesen, das accounting (= general accounting rules and regulations)

Reiseaufwendungen (*pl*) travel expenses

Reisekosten (*pl*) travel expenses

Restlaufzeit, die (-en) remaining period/residual time to maturity (= time period to date of payment)

Risiken aus schwebenden Geschäften risks with contractual commitments/pending projects

Risiko, das (-ken) risk

Rohstoff, der (-e) raw material

Rücklage, die (-n) reserve (= set aside fund)

Rücklage für eigene Anteile reserve for own shares*

Rückstellung, die provision [accrual] (= estimate of expected future charge or anticipated future loss, exact amount and timing not yet known; long-term or short-term item)

Rückstellung für latente Steuern provision for deferred taxation

Rückstellungen (*pl*) provisions for liabilities and charges* [accruals] (= estimates of expected future charges and anticipated future losses, exact amount and timing not yet known; long-term and short-term items)

Rückstellungen für Pensionen und ähnliche Verpflichtungen provisions for pensions and similar obligations

Rückstellungen für Risiken aus schwebendenen Geschäften provisions for risks with contractual commitments/pending projects

Rückstellungen für Steuern provisions for taxation

Rückstellungen für ungewisse Verbindlichkeiten provisions for probable charges

S

Sachanlage, die (-n) tangible fixed asset

Sachkosten für Geschäftsräume fixtures and fittings

Sachkosten für Personalausbildung costs of materials for staff training

saldieren to balance off (an account)/to net off

Saldo, der (-den) account balance/balance/net position

Satz, der (-ätze) rate

Satzung, die memorandum and articles of association [charter and bylaws] (= a company's own rules)

satzungsgemäß in conformity with memorandum and/or articles of association [in conformity with charter and/or bylaws].

satzungsmäßig in conformity with memorandum and/or articles of association [in conformity with charter and/or bylaws]

satzungsmäßige Rücklage reserve provided for by the articles of association* [statutory reserve/reserve required by corporation bylaws]

Schadensersatzanspruch, der (-üche) compensation claim/claim for damages

Scheck, der (-s) cheque

Schema, das (-ta) format

Schuldverschreibung, die (-en) debenture (= a company's written acknowledgement of a debt, similar to a loan)

Schutzrechte (pl) industrial property rights (e.g. patents)

schwebende Geschäfte contractual commitments/pending projects (= both parties to a contract have not yet met their respective obligations, no goods/services or money have as yet been transferred)

Sicherheit, die (-en) security

Sicherheiten für Verbindlichkeiten securities for creditors

Sonderabschreibung, die (-en) special depreciation required or permitted by German tax legislation (in excess of the normal depreciation charges)

Sonderposten, der (-) special post/position/item

Sonderposten mit Rücklageanteil special tax-allowable reserve (= contains retained profits as well as the respective tax payable)

sonstig other, sundry

sonstige betriebliche Aufwendungen other operating charges*

sonstige betriebliche Erträge other operating income* [other operating revenue]

sonstige Finanzanlagen other long-term investments

sonstige Gemeinkosten sundry overheads

sonstige Rückstellungen other provisions*

sonstige Steuern other taxes

sonstige Vermögensgegenstände (pl) other current assets

sonstige Wertpapiere other investments*

sonstige Zinsen und ähnliche Erträge other interest receivable and similar income*

soziale Abgaben social security costs*

soziale Aufwendungen social security costs

soziale Sicherheit social security

Sozialkosten (pl) social security costs

Sozialplan, der (-äne) social fund for employees (to compensate employees affected by changes in business operations, e.g. plant closure or change in plant location)

Stammaktie, die (-n) ordinary share/equity share [common share/stock/equity]

Stammkapital, das share capital (in GmbH)

Stand am (e.g. Stand am 31.12.1993) as at (e.g. as at 31.12.1993)

Steuer, die (-n) tax

Steuerabgrenzungsposten, der (-) (*aktiv*) prepaid tax

Steuerbilanz, die (-en) tax balance sheet

steuerfreie Rücklagen tax-free reserves (profits tansferred into these reserves are temporarily not taxed)

Steuergutschrift, die (-en) tax credit

steuerliche Sonderabschreibungen special depreciation required or permitted by German tax legislation (in excess of the normal depreciation charges)

Steuern vom Einkommen und vom Ertrag taxes on profit [taxes on income]

Steuerrecht, das law of taxation

steuerrechtlich as per tax law

Steuerrückstellung, die (-en) tax provision

T

tätigen to effect/to make (sales)

technisch technical, industrial

technische Anlagen plant and machinery (e.g. technical equipment, factory machines, tools)

Telefonkosten (*pl*) telephone costs

testieren to sign (the auditor)

thesaurierte Gewinne accumulated profits

Tilgung, die (-en) redemption/repayment/paying back/paying off

Tochtergesellschaft, die (-en) subsidiary/subsidiary undertaking

U

Überschuß, der (-üsse) surplus

übersteigen to exceed

Überziehungskredit, der (-e) overdraft/overdraft facility

übrige Aufwendungen sundry expenses

übrige Aufwendungen für Roh-, Hilfs- und Betriebsstoffe other costs of raw materials and consumables

übrige betriebliche Aufwendungen sundry operating charges

übrige betriebliche Erträge sundry operating income

umbuchen to transfer (to another account), to reclassify, to repost

Umbuchung, die (-en) transfer (to another account)

Umlaufvermögen, das current assets

umrechnen to translate (currencies), to convert

Umsatz, der sales volume, sales revenue, turnover

Umsätze (*pl*) sales/turnover

Umsatzeinbußen (*pl*) decrease in turnover/sales

Umsatzerlöse (*pl*) turnover*/sales/sales revenues

Umsatzkosten (*pl*) cost of sales (= cost of goods sold)

Umsatzsteuer, die value-added tax

Umsatzzuwachs, der increase in turnover/sales

Umtausch, der (einer Anleihe) conversion (e.g. conversion of a loan into ordinary shares)

umtauschen to convert (a security), to convert (a currency)

uneinbringliche Forderungen bad debts/irrecoverable debts [uncollectible receivables]

unfertige Erzeugnisse work-in-progress*[work-in-process], unfinished goods

unfertige Leistungen work-in-progress* [work-in-process], uncompleted services

ungewisse Verbindlichkeiten probable (= expected) charges

Unternehmen, das (-) business, firm, undertaking [enterprise] (= any form of business)

Unterstützung, die (-en) support/aid/assistance

unverrechnete Lieferungen und Leistungen goods and services (account) not yet balanced off

Urlaubsentgelt, das (-e) holiday payment [vacation pay]

Urlaubsgehalt, das (-älter) holiday payment [vacation pay]

V

Veranschaulichung, die (-en) illustration

veranschlagen to calculate, to estimate

veräußern to sell/to dispose of (assets, investments)

Verbindlichkeit, die obligation, liability

Verbindlichkeiten (*pl*) creditors [accounts payable/payable(s)]

Verbindlichkeiten aus der Annahme gezogener Wechsel und der Ausstellung eigener Wechsel (net) bills of exchange payable [liabilities on bills accepted and drawn]

Verbindlichkeiten aus Lieferungen und Leistungen trade creditors* [trade payables]

Verbindlichkeiten gegenüber Kreditinstituten bank loans and overdrafts*

Verbindlichkeiten gegenüber Unternehmen, mit denen ein Beteiligungsverhältnis besteht amounts owed to undertakings in which the company has a participating interest* [payable to enterprises in which participations are held]

Verbindlichkeiten gegenüber verbundenen Unternehmen amounts owed to group undertakings [payable to affiliated enterprises]

Verbindlichkeiten mit einer Restlaufzeit von mehr als einem Jahr creditors [liabilities] falling due after more than one year

verbrauchen to consume, to use (up)

verbundenes Unternehmen group undertaking, subsidiary undertaking [affiliated enterprise]

Verkauf, der (-äufe) sale

verkaufen to sell/to dispose of (assets, investments)

Verkaufskontrakt, der (-e) sales contract

Verkaufsprovisionen (*pl*) sales commission

Verlust, der (-e) loss

Verluste aus dem Abgang von Gegenständen des Anlagevermögens losses on the disposal of (any type of) fixed assets

Verluste aus Wertminderungen und der Ausbuchung von Forderungen losses from doubtful and bad debts (= expected losses from probable and certain non-payment of debtors)

Verlustvortrag, der (-äge) loss carried/brought forward (= previous years' losses accumulated)

vermieten to let/to rent out [to hire out]/to lease

vermietete Erzeugnisse manufactured assets rented out, manufactured equipment leased to customers

Verminderung, die (-en) decrease

Verminderung des Bestands an fertigen und unfertigen Erzeugnissen decrease in stocks of finished goods and in work-in-progress [decrease in finished inventories and in work-in-process]

Vermögens-, Finanz- und Ertragslage position of assets, finances and profits

Vermögensgegenstand, der (-ände) asset

Vermögenslage, die asset position

Vermögensseite, die assets side

Vermögensteuer, die tax on assets

vernünftige kaufmännische Beurteilung sound commercial judgement

Veröffentlichungspflicht, die requirement to publish (accounts)

Verpflichtung, die (-en) obligation, commitment

verrechnen to set/net off (against), to balance off, to charge (as an expense), to allocate/apportion (production costs), to clear (a cheque)

Verschmelzung, die merger

Versicherung, die (-en) insurance

Versicherungsgeschäft, das (-e) insurance business, underwriting business

versicherungstechnische Aufwendungen insurance costs

versicherungstechnische Rückstellung provision for insurances

Versicherungsteuer, die tax on insurances

Versorgungsleistung, die (-en) provision of social benefits

Verteilung, die (-en) distribution, allocation, apportionment

Vertriebsaufwendungen (*pl*) distribution costs* (= selling expenses)

Verwaltungs- und Vertriebskosten administrative expenses and distribution costs

Verwaltungsaufwendungen (*pl*)
administrative expenses*

verzinslich interest-bearing

Vorauszahlung, die (-en)
prepayment/payment in advance

Vorfinanzierung, die (-en) advance
financing

Vorräte (*pl*) stock(s) [inventory (-ies)]

Vorrechtsaktie, die (-en) preference
share [preferred stock]

Vorschrift, die (-en) rule, regulation

Vorschrift, gesetzliche legal requirement

Vorstand, der (-ände) board of directors
[management board] (AG)

Vortrag, der (-äge) (amount) carried
forward, (amount) brought forward

vorzeitige Pensionierung early retirement

Vorzugsaktie, die (-n) preference share
[preferred stock]

W

Währung, die (-en) currency

Währungs- und Kursgewinne gains on
foreign exchange transactions (= gains
from exchange rate fluctuations)

Währungs- und Kursverluste losses on
foreign exchange transactions (= losses
from exchange rate fluctuations)

Währungsumrechnung, die (-en)
foreign currency translation

Währungsumtausch, der conversion of a
currency

Ware, die goods [merchandise]

Ware liefern to deliver goods
[merchandise]

Waren (*pl*) goods for resale [merchandise]/
goods/commodities/products

Waren zum Wiederverkauf goods for
resale [merchandise]

Wechsel, der (-) bill of exchange

Wechsel akzeptieren to accept a bill of
exchange (= to countersign a bill of
exchange)

Wechsel annehmen to accept a bill of
exchange (= to countersign a bill of
exchange)

Wechsel ausstellen to draw/make out a
bill of exchange

Wechselkurs, der (-e) exchange rate

Wechselsteuer, die tax on bills of
exchange

Welthandel, der world trade

Weltkonjunktur, die world economy

Weltumsatz, der (-ätze) world
turnover/world sales

Werbekosten (*pl*) advertising costs (=
marketing and advertising)

Wert, der (-e) value

Wertansatz, der determination of
value/valuation

Wertberichtigung, die (-en) adjustment
to asset/special additional depreciation
on fixed or current asset (permitted by
German tax law)

**Wertberichtigung zum
Anlagevermögen** special additional
depreciation on fixed assets (=
adjustment permitted by German tax
law)

**Wertberichtigung zum
Umlaufvermögen** special additional
write-off on debtors (= adjustment
permitted by German tax law)

Wertminderung, die (-en) reduction in
value/diminution in value

Wertpapier, das (-e) investment*/
security (= stocks, shares, debentures,
bonds, loan notes etc.)

Wertpapiere des Anlagevermögens 1.
long-term investments (= investments in
the fixed asset section), 2. certain
long-term investments (e.g. small
investments)

Wertpapiere des Umlaufvermögens
short-term investments [securities]
(= investments in the current asset
section)

Wertverlust, der (-e) diminution/loss in
value

Wiederbeschaffungskosten (*pl*)
replacement costs

Wiederherstellungskosten (*pl*)
reproduction costs

Wirtschaftsentwicklung, die economic
development

Wirtschaftsgut, das (-üter) business
asset

Wirtschaftsindikatoren (*pl*) economic
indicators (e.g. rate of inflation,
unemployment)

Wirtschaftslage, die economic
situation/position

Wirtschaftsprüfer, der (-) auditor

Z

Zinsaufwendungen (*pl*) interest payable
Zinsen (*pl*) interest
Zinsen und ähnliche Aufwendungen
  interest payable and similar charges*
Zinsen und ähnliche Erträge interest
  receivable and similar income
Zinsergebnis, das net interest (= interest
  receivable less interest payable)
Zinserträge (*pl*) interest receivable
Zinszahlung, die (-en) interest payment
zu Buche schlagen to affect
Zugänge (*pl*) additions

Zulage, die (-n) employee bonus/extra
  pay, grant, contribution
Zuschuß, der (-üsse) contribution, grant,
  subsidy
**Zuschüsse und Zulagen für Forschung
  und Entwicklung** contributions and
  grants for research and development
zustandekommen to be arrived at (a profit)
Zwischenabschluß, der (-üsse) interim
  accounts/interim report/interim
  financial statements
zweifelhafte Forderungen (*pl*) doubtful
  debts [doubtful accounts receivable]

English–German

A

accept, to (bill of exchange) (= countersigning a bill of exchange) annehmen/akzeptieren

account balance Saldo, der (-den)

accounting (= general accounting rules and regulations) Rechnungswesen, das

accounting period Abrechnungszeitraum, der (-äume)

accounting policy (if basic principle of accounting) Bilanzierungsgrundsatz, der (-ätze)

accounting policy (if method of valuation) Bewertungsgrundsatz, der (-ätze)

accounting policies Bilanzierungs- und Bewertungsgrundsätze (*pl*)

accounting principles Rechnungsgrundsätze (*pl*)

accounting year Berichtsjahr, das (-e)/Rechnungsjahr, das (-e)

account payable [US] (= creditor) 1. Verbindlichkeit, die (-en), 2. Gläubiger, der (-)

account receivable [US] 1. Forderung, die (-en), 2. Kunde, der (-n)

accounts (= financial statements) Abschluß, der (-üsse)/Jahresbericht, der (-e)

accrual (= outstanding payment or estimate of expected future expense, exact amount and timing not yet known – short-term item) Rechnungsabgrenzungsposten, der (-) (*passiv*), ausstehende Rechnung

accruals [US] (= estimates of expected future charges and anticipated future losses, exact amount and timing not yet known) Rückstellungen (*pl*)

accrue, to (e.g. costs) anfallen (*sep*)

accrued income (= income due but not yet received at balance sheet date) Rechnungsabgrenzungsposten, der (-) (*aktiv*)

accumulate, to (e.g. interest) anfallen (*sep*)

accumulated kumuliert, thesauriert

accumulated depreciation (= total of depreciation charged so far) kumulierte Abschreibungen

to acquire erwerben

acquisition costs Anschaffungskosten (*pl*)

additions Zugänge (*pl*)

adjustment Berichtigung, die (-en)

administrative expenses* Verwaltungsaufwendungen (*pl*)

administrative expenses and distribution costs Verwaltungs- und Vertriebskosten (*pl*)

advance financing Vorfinanzierung, die (-en)

advance payment Anzahlung, die (-en)

advertising costs (= marketing and advertising) Werbekosten (*pl*)

affect, to zu Buche schlagen

affiliated enterprise [US] verbundenes Unternehmen

allocate, to belegen mit

allocation (of costs) Verteilung, die (-en)

amortisation (= term for depreciation of intangible assets) Abschreibung, die (-en)

amortisation of intangible fixed assets Abschreibungen auf immaterielle Vermögensgegenstände

amount to, to belaufen, auf (*refl*)

amount brought forward Vortrag, der (-äge)

amount carried forward Vortrag, der (-äge)

amount of coverage Deckungsbetrag, der (-äge)

(amounts) falling due after more than five years mit einer Restlaufzeit über fünf Jahre

(amounts) falling due after more than one year mit einer Restlaufzeit von mehr als einem Jahr

(amounts) falling due within one year mit einer Restlaufzeit bis zu einem Jahr

amounts owed by undertakings in which the company has a participating interest* Forderungen gegen Unternehmen, mit denen ein Beteiligungsverhältnis besteht

amounts owed by group undertakings* Forderungen gegen verbundene Unternehmen

amounts owed to undertakings in which the company has a participating interest* Verbindlichkeiten gegenüber Unternehmen, mit denen ein Beteiligungsverhältnis besteht

amounts owed to group undertakings* Verbindlichkeiten gegenüber verbundenen Unternehmen

amounts written off (investments) Abschreibung, die (-en)

amounts written off investments (i.e. long-term and short-term investments) Abschreibungen auf Finanzanlagen und auf Wertpapiere des Umlaufvermögens

ancillary business activity Nebengeschäft, das (-e)

anniversary award (to employees) Jubiläumszuwendung, die (-en)

anniversary gift (to employees) Jubiläumszuwendung, die (-en)

annual accounts Jahresabschluß, der (-üsse)

annual financial statements Jahresabschluß, der (-üsse)

annual report Jahresabschluß, der (-üsse)

annual report preparation costs Jahresabschlußkosten (*pl*)

apportion, to (e.g. production costs) verrechnen

apportionment Verteilung, die

arise, to (e.g. costs) anfallen (*sep*)

articles of association (of a company) (= company's own rules) Satzung, die (-en)

as at (e.g. as at 31.12.1993) Stand am (z.B. Stand am 31.12.1993)

asset Vermögensgegenstand, der (-ände)

assets (= all items on the left-hand side of a German balance sheet) Aktiva (*pl*)/Vermögen, das/Vermögensgegenstände (*pl*)

assets in the course of construction Anlagen im Bau

associated company assoziierte Kapitalgesellschaft

associated undertaking assoziiertes Unternehmen

audit Abschlußprüfung, die (-en)

audit, to prüfen/auditieren (books of accounts)

audit opinion Bestätigungsvermerk, der

auditor Abschlußprüfer, der (-)/Wirtschaftsprüfer, der (-)

audit report Bestätigungsvermerk, der

authorised capital (= additional share capital authorised for future issue) genehmigtes Kapital

average exchange rate Durchschnittskurs, der (-e)

B

bad debt Forderungsausfall, der (-älle)/uneinbringliche Forderung, die (-en)

bad debts written off ausgebuchte Forderungen

balance (of an account) Saldo, der (-den)

balance, to (e.g. an account) bilanzieren

balance off, to verrechnen

balance sheet Bilanz, die (-en)

balance sheet profit (=current year profit adjusted for the balance sheet) Bilanzgewinn, der

bank Kreditinstitut, das (-e)/Bank, die (-en)

bank charges Bankspesen (*pl*)

bank fees Bankspesen (*pl*)

bank loan Bankdarlehen, das (-)/Darlehen, das (-)

bank loans and overdrafts* Verbindlichkeiten gegenüber Kreditinstituten

bankruptcy Konkurs, der (-e)

basis of calculation Kalkulationsbasis, die

bearer share (= share in bearer form is owned by the person in whose possession the share-certificate is; it is freely transferable, e.g. ordinary and preference shares in AG – rare in UK) Inhaberaktie, die (-n)

bill [US] Rechnung, die (-en)

bill of exchange Wechsel, der (-)

board of directors Vorstand, der (in AG), Geschäftsführer (*pl*) (in GmbH)

bond Anleihe, die (-n)/Schuldverschreibung, die (-en)

bonus Bonus, der (-ni)

book value (= original cost less accumulated depreciation) Buchwert, der (-e)

bought-in goods bezogene Waren

bought-in services bezogene Leistungen

branch Filiale, die (-n)

brand (with foods) Marke, die (-n)
brand product Markenartikel, der (-)
buildings Bauten (*pl*)
buildings on third-party land Bauten auf fremden Grundstücken
business 1. Unternehmen, das (-)/ Geschäftsbetrieb, der (-e), 2. Gewerbe, das, (-)
business activity Geschäftsverlauf, der
business asset Wirtschaftsgut, das (-üter)
business establishment (= sum total of business activities) Geschäftsbetrieb, der (-e)
business expansion costs Aufwendungen für die Erweiterung des Geschäftsbetriebs
business transaction Geschäftsvorfall, der (-älle)
buying rate of a currency Geldkurs, der
by-product Nebenprodukt, das (-e)

C

calculate, to verrechnen, kalkulieren
calculation of inventory [US] Beständerechnung, die (-en)
calculation of profit Gewinnermittlung, die
calculation of stock Beständerechnung, die (-en)
capital 1. (= share capital) gezeichnetes Kapital, 2. (= share capital and reserves) Eigenkapital, das
capital and liabilities (= all items on the right-hand side of a German balance sheet) Passiva (*pl*)
capital and liabilities side Kapitalseite, die (-n)
capital and reserves (= shareholders' fund) Eigenkapital, das
capital reserve (= mainly accumulated share premiums) Kapitalrücklage, die (-n)
capitalise, to aktivieren
capitalised costs aktivierte Aufwendungen
capitalised in-house output [US] (= internally produced and capitalised assets) aktivierte Eigenleistungen
capital yields tax [US] (= tax on dividends, interest, etc.) Kapitalertragsteuer, die

cash Bargeld, das
cash at bank (= credit-balance in bank account) Bankguthaben, das (-)
cash at bank and in hand* flüssige Mittel (*pl*)/Bankguthaben und Kassenbestände
cash in hand Geldbestand, der (-ände)/ Kassenbestand, der (-ände)
cash in the till Kassenbestand, der (-ände)
cash resources Geldmittel (*pl*)
central bank deposit Bundesbankguthaben, das (-)
change in finished inventories and in work-in-process [US] Veränderung des Bestands an fertigen und unfertigen Erzeugnissen
change in stocks of finished goods and in work-in-progress* Veränderung des Bestands an fertigen und unfertigen Erzeugnissen
charge, to (e.g. an account) abrechnen/verrechnen
charges Aufwendungen (*pl*)
charges related to participations Beteiligungsaufwendungen (*pl*)
charter and bylaws [US] (= a company's own rules) Satzung, die (-en)
cheque Scheck, der (-s)
chief executive Geschäftsführer, der (-)
clear, to (e.g. a cheque) abrechnen/verrechnen
client Kunde, der (-n)
closure Einstellung, die (-en)/ Schließung, die (-en)
closure costs Aufwendungen für Schließungen
commerce Handel, der
commercial gewerblich
commercial balance sheet Handelsbilanz, die (-en)
commercial law Handelsrecht, das
commission Provision, die (-en)
commodities Güter (*pl*)
commodity Gut, das
common equity [US] (= ordinary share) Stammaktie, die (-n)
common stock [US] (= ordinary share) Stammaktie, die (-n)
company (= type of business organisation which constitutes a legal person separate from its owners) Kapitalgesellschaft, die (-en)

company health insurance fund
Betriebskrankenkasse, die (-n)

compensation claim
Schadensersatzanspruch, der (-üche)

compulsory information Pflichtangaben (*pl*)

compulsory winding up Konkurs, der (-e)

compute, to (e.g. taxes) ermitteln

concession Konzession, die (-en)

conditional (authorised unissued) **capital** (= additional share capital authorised for future issue conditional on conversion rights or share options being exercised) bedingtes Kapital

consolidate, to (= to combine the financial statements of several businesses into one set of accounts) konsolidieren

consolidated retained earnings [US] Konzerngewinn, der

construction Bau, der

construction industry Baubranche, die

consumables (e.g. single-use factory materials, small tools) Hilfs- und Betriebsstoffe (*pl*)

contingent liability
Eventualverbindlichkeit, die (-en)

contractual commitments (= both parties to a contract have not yet met their respective obigations, no goods/services or money have as yet been transferred) schwebende Geschäfte

contribution Beitrag, der (-äge)

contribution for occupational accident insurance
Berufsgenossenschaftsbeitrag, der (-äge)

contributions and grants for research and development Zuschüsse und Zulagen für Forschung und Entwicklung

conversion (e.g. conversion of a loan into shares, conversion of a currency) Umtausch/Konversion (einer Anleihe), Währungsumtausch

conversion right (e.g. right to exchange a loan for shares in the same company) Umtauschrecht, das (-e)/ Konversionsrecht, das (-e)

convert, to (e.g. a currency, a security) umrechnen, umtauschen/konvertieren

convertible konvertibel

corporate management report [US] Lagebericht, der (-e)

corporate tax [US] (= tax on business profits) Körperschaftsteuer, die

corporation [US] (= type of business organisation which constitutes a legal person separate from its owners) Kapitalgesellschaft, die (-en)

corporation income tax [US] (= tax on business profits) Körperschaftsteuer, die

corporation tax (= tax on business profits) Körperschaftsteuer, die (-en)

correction Berichtigung, die (-en)

cost of manufacture Herstellungskosten (*pl*)

cost of materials Materialaufwand, der (-ände)

cost of production Herstellungskosten (*pl*)

cost of purchased/bought-in goods
Aufwendungen für bezogene Waren

cost of raw materials and consumables
Aufwendungen für Roh-, Hilfs- und Betriebsstoffe

cost of sales (= cost of goods sold) Umsatzkosten/Herstellungskosten

cost price Herstellungspreis, der (-e)

cost(s) Aufwendungen (*pl*)

course of business Geschäftsablauf, der (-äufe)

coverage Deckung, die

credit, to (= to enter on the credit/right side of an account) gutbringen (*sep*)/gutschreiben (*sep*)

credit balance (= deposit at bank) Guthaben, das (-)

creditor 1. Verbindlichkeit, die (-en), 2. Gläubiger, der (-)

creditors Verbindlichkeiten (*pl*)

creditors falling due after more than one year Verbindlichkeiten mit einer Restlaufzeit von mehr als einem Jahr

currency Währung, die (-en)

current account (at a bank) Girokonto, das (-ten)

current asset investment (= short-term investment) Wertpapier des Umlaufvermögens

current asset items Gegenstände des Umlaufvermögens

current assets* Umlaufvermögen, das

customer Kunde, der (-n)
customs duty on exports Ausfuhrzoll, der (-ölle)

D

debenture (= a company's written acknowledgement of a debt, similar to a loan) Schuldverschreibung, die (-en)/Anleihe, die (-en)
debenture loans Anleihen
debit, to (= to enter on the debit/left side of an account) buchen, zu Lasten (*gen*)
debtor 1. Forderung, die (-en), 2. Kunde, der (-n)
debtors and other current assets Forderungen und sonstige Vermögensgegenstände
debtors for goods delivered and services rendered Forderungen aus Lieferungen und Leistungen
debtors from the insurance business Forderungen aus dem Versicherungsgeschäft
debtors written off (= bad debts written off) ausgebuchte Forderungen
decrease Verminderung, die (-en)
decrease in sales Umsatzeinbußen (*pl*)
decrease in turnover Umsatzeinbußen (*pl*)
deduct, to absetzen (*sep*)
deferred income (= income received but relating to future accounting period) Rechnungsabgrenzungsposten, der (-) (*passiv*)
deferred tax latente Steuern
delivery Lieferung, die (-en)
deposit 1. Guthaben, das, 2. Anzahlung, die (-en)
depreciation Abschreibung, die (-en)
depreciation rate Abschreibungssatz, der (-ätze)
depreciation method Abschreibungsmethode, die (-en)
determine, to (a value, a profit) ansetzen (*sep*), ermitteln
determination of profit Gewinnermittlung, die
determination of value Wertansatz, der
diminution in value Wertverlust, der (-e)
director Geschäftsführer, der (-)
directors' report Lagebericht, der (-e)

discontinuance Einstellung, die (-en)
discount (e.g. cash discount) Nachlaß, der
discount on investment Disagio, das
disposals Abgänge (*pl*)
dispose of, to (assets, investments) verkaufen/veräußern
distribution 1. Verteilung, die, (-en), 2. Vertrieb, der
distribution costs* Vertriebsaufwendungen (*pl*)
distribution of profits Gewinnausschüttung, die (-en)
dividend Dividende, die (-, -n)
dividend payment (= distribution of profits to shareholders) Gewinnausschüttung, die (-en)/Ausschüttung, die (-en)
doubtful accounts receivable [US] zweifelhafte Forderungen (*pl*)
doubtful and bad debts (= probable and certain non-payment of debtors) Wertminderung und Ausbuchung von Forderungen
doubtful debt provision Forderungswertberichtigung, die (-en)
doubtful debts zweifelhafte Forderungen (*pl*)
down payment Anzahlung, die (-en)
draft (= bill of exchange drawn but not yet accepted by the other party) gezogener Wechsel
draw, to (bill of exchange) ziehen, ausstellen
draw, to (money from bank account) abheben
drop in profits Gewinnrückgang, der

E

early retirement vorzeitige Pensionierung
earnings Gewinn, der (-e)
economic development Wirtschaftsentwicklung, die
economic indicators (e.g. rate of inflation, unemployment) Wirtschaftsindikatoren (*pl*)
economic situation Wirtschaftslage, die
effect, to (e.g. sales) tätigen
employee Arbeitnehmer, der (-)
employee discount Arbeitnehmer-Rabatt, der (-e)

employer Arbeitgeber, der (-)

employment costs Personalaufwand, der/Personalkosten (*pl*)

enterprise [US] Unternehmen, das (-)/ Geschäftsbetrieb, der (-e)

entry (= item in balance sheet/profit and loss account/individual account) Posten, der (-)/Eintragung, die (-en)/ Buchung, die (-en)

equity (= shareholders' fund/capital and reserves) Eigenkapital, das

equity holder [US] Aktionär, der (-e) (in AG), Gesellschafter, der (-) (in GmbH), Anteilseigner, der, (-) (in GmbH)

equity share (= ordinary share) Stammaktie, die (-n)

estimate, to veranschlagen

exceed, to übersteigen

exceptional depreciation (= in excess of the normal depreciation charge) außerplanmäßige Abschreibung

exchange rate Wechselkurs, der (-e)

exchange rate gain Kursgewinn, der (-e)

exchange rate gains on foreign currencies Fremdwährungskursgewinne (*pl*)

expansion Erweiterung, die (-en)

expenditure Ausgaben (*pl*)

explanations Erläuterungen (*pl*)

export/exports Ausfuhr, die

extraordinary charges* außerordentliche Aufwendungen

extraordinary income* außerordentliche Erträge

extraordinary profit or loss* außerordentliches Ergebnis

extraordinary result außerordentliches Ergebnis

F

fall due, to anfallen (*sep*)

financial assets [US] (= long-term investments) Finanzanlagen (*pl*)

financial period Abrechnungszeitraum, der (-äume)

financial position Finanzlage, die

financial year Rechnungsjahr, das (-e)/ Berichtsjahr, das (-e)

financing Finanzierung, die

finished goods fertige Erzeugnisse

fixed asset investment (= long-term investment) Finanzanlage, die (-n)

fixed asset items Gegenstände des Anlagevermögens

fixed asset movement schedule Anlagenspiegel, der (-)

fixed asset schedule Anlagenspiegel, der (-)

fixed assets* Anlagevermögen, das

fixed-interest bearing festverzinslich

fixed-interest bearing investment festverzinsliches Wertpapier

fixtures and fittings Geschäftsraumausstattung, die (-en)/ Geschäftsausstattung, die (-en)

fixtures and fittings of a plant Betriebsausstattung, die (-en)

foreign currency Fremdwährung, die (-en)

foreign currency translation Währungsumrechnung, die (-en)

foreign exchange transaction Währungsumtausch, der

foreign market Auslandsmarkt, der (-ärkte)

format Format, das (-e)

franchise Konzession, die (-en)

funds Geldmittel (*pl*)

G

gain Gewinn, der (-e)

gains on foreign exchange transactions (= gains from exchange rate fluctuations) Währungs- und Kursgewinne

Generally Accepted Accounting Principles (GAAP) Grundsätze ordnungsmäßiger Buchführung (GoB)

German central bank Bundesbank, die

goods Waren (*pl*)/Güter (*pl*)

goods for resale Waren zum Wiederverkauf

goodwill* (= worth of a business over and above its actual assets) Firmenwert, der (-e)/Geschäftswert, der (-e)

grant Zuschuß, der (-üsse)/Zulage, die (-n)

group (= parent undertaking and its subsidiaries) Konsolierungskreis, der (-e)/ Konzern, der (-e)

group of undertakings Konsolierungskreis, der (-e)/Konzern, der (-e)

119

group undertaking (= subsidiary or parent undertaking) verbundes Unternehmen

group profit Konzerngewinn, der

guarantee Bürgschaft, die (-en)

guarantee obligation Garantieverpflichtung, die (-en)

guaranty [US] Bürgschaft, die (-en)

H

hire out, to [US] vermieten

holiday payment Urlaubsgehalt, das (-älter)/Urlaubsentgelt, das (-e)

I

illustration Veranschaulichung, die (-en)

in real (= money) **terms** real

income (from) Erträge (aus)

income from participating interest (= dividends and similar income) Erträge aus Beteiligungen

income from shares in affiliated enterprises [US] Erträge aus Beteiligungen an verbundenen Unternehmen

income from shares in group undertakings Erträge aus Beteiligungen an verbundenen Unternehmen

income from other investments and long-term loans Erträge aus anderen Wertpapieren und Ausleihungen des Finanzanlagevermögens

income from the disposal of (tangible) fixed assets Erträge aus dem Abgang von Gegenständen des Sachanlagevermögens

income statement [US] Erfolgsrechnung, die (-en)/Gewinn- und Verlustrechnung, die (-en)

incorporated business (= company) Kapitalgesellschaft, die (-en)

increase in turnover Umsatzzuwachs, der

industrial industriell, gewerblich

industrialised country Industrieland, das (-änder)

industrial property rights (e.g. patents, design patents, trademarks) gewerbliche Schutzrechte/Schutzrechte (*pl*)

industry 1. Industrie, die (-en), 2. Gewerbe, das (-)

Inland Revenue Finanzamt, das (-ämter)/Finanzbehörde, die (-n)

input value (= original cost of purchase/manufacture) Einstandswert, der (-e)

insurance Versicherung, die (-en)

insurance business Versicherungsgeschäft, das (-e)

insurance costs versicherungstechnische Aufwendungen

intangible assets* immaterielle Vermögensgegenstände

interest Zinsen (*pl*)

interest-bearing verzinslich

interest in a company Anteil an einer Kapitalgesellschaft

interest payable Zinsaufwendungen (*pl*)

interest payable and similar charges* Zinsen und ähnliche Aufwendungen

interest payment Zinszahlung, die (-en)

interest receivable Zinserträge (*pl*)

interest receivable and similar income Zinsen und ähnliche Erträge

interim accounts Zwischenabschluß, der (-üsse)

interim financial statements Zwischenabschluß, der (-üsse)

interim report Zwischenabschluß, der (-üsse)

internal turnover (e.g. within a group, between branches) Innenumsatzerlöse (*pl*)

inventories Vorräte (*pl*)/Bestand, der/Bestände (*pl*)

inventory Vorräte (*pl*)/Bestand, der

inventory changes [US] (= change in finished inventories and in work-in-process) Bestandsveränderungen (*pl*)

inventory taking Bestandsaufnahme, die (-n)

investment (e.g. stocks and shares, loan-notes, bonds, etc.) Wertpapier, das (-e)/Kapitalanlage, die (-n)/Kapital, das

investments* (in fixed-asset section) Finanzanlagen (*pl*)

investments* (in current-asset section) Wertpapiere des Umlaufvermögens

investor Anleger, der (-)

invoice Rechnung, die (-en)
invoice, to (e.g. goods or services)
  abrechnen
invoiced (sales of) services
  abgerechnete Leistungen
irrecoverable debts uneinbringliche
  Forderungen
issue, to (shares) ausgeben/emittieren
issue of a patent Patentierung, die (-en)
issue of shares Aktienemission, die (-en)
items from tangible fixed assets
  Gegenstände des Sachanlagevermögens

L

land Grundstück, das (-e)
law of taxation Steuerrecht, das
lease (on land or buildings) Pacht, die
lease, to verpachten
lease prepayment Pachtvorauszahlung,
  die (-en)
lease property Pachtgrundstück, das (-e)
leasehold properties/property
  Pachtgrundstücke (*pl*)/
  grundstücksgleiche Bauten
leasehold rights grundstücksgleiche
  Rechte
leasing (provides long-term use of an
  asset without legal ownership)
  Leasing, das
leasing obligations
  Leasingverpflichtungen (*pl*)
legal entity juristische Person, die
legal form of a business (e.g. AG, GmbH,
  etc.) Unternehmensform, die (-en)
legal liability Haftung, die
legal person juristische Person, die
legal reserve (= reserve required by law,
  AktG) gesetzliche Rücklage
legal requirement gesetzliche Vorschrift
liabilities (= creditors, provisions and
  accruals) Fremdkapital, das
liabilities (= creditors) [US]
  Verbindlichkeiten (*pl*)
liabilities and shareholders' equity (= all
  creditors and capital and reserves)
  [US] Passiva (*pl*)
**liabilities on bills (of exchange)
  accepted and drawn** [US]
  Verbindlichkeiten aus der Annahme
  gezogener Wechsel und der
  Ausstellung eigener Wechsel

licence Konzession, die (-en)
license [US] Konzession, die (-en)
liquidate, to liquidieren
liquidation (= winding-up of a business)
  Liquidation, die (-en)
liquid funds flüssige Mittel (*pl*)
listing Auflistung, die (-en)
loan Ausleihung, die (-en)/Anleihe, die
  (-n)/Schuldverschreibung, die (-en)
loans to affiliated enterprises [US]
  Ausleihungen an verbundene
  Unternehmen
**loans to enterprises in which
  participations are held** [US]
  Ausleihungen an Unternehmen, mit
  denen ein Beteiligungsverhältnis besteht
**loans to undertakings in which the
  company has a participating interest***
  Ausleihungen an Unternehmen, mit
  denen ein Beteiligungsverhältnis besteht
loans to group undertakings*
  Ausleihungen an verbundene
  Unternehmen
long-term loans Ausleihungen des
  Finanzanlagevermögens
loss Verlust, der (-e)
loss brought forward (= previous years'
  losses accumulated) Verlustvortrag,
  der (-äge)
loss for the financial year
  Jahresfehlbetrag, der
net loss for the year [US]
  Jahresfehlbetrag, der
loss attributable to minority interests
  (i.e. minority shareholders) auf
  konzernfremde Gesellschafter
  entfallender Verlust
loss of receivable outstanding [US]
  Forderungsausfall, der (-älle)
**losses on foreign exchange
  transactions** (= losses from exchange
  rate fluctuations) Währungs- und
  Kursverluste
losses on the disposal of fixed assets
  Verluste aus dem Abgang von
  Gegenständen des Anlagevermögens
loss transfer Verlustübernahme, die (-n)

M

make (with industrial goods, e.g. cars)
  Marke, die (-n)

make, to (an entry in the accounts)
buchen

make, to (a down/advance payment)
anzahlen

management board [US] Vorstand, der
(-ände)

manager Geschäftsführer, der (-)

manufactured assets Erzeugnisse (*pl*)

manufactured good/item/product
Erzeugnis, das (-se)

manufacturer Hersteller, der (-)

manufacturing business
produzierendes Gewerbe

manufacturing costs Herstellungskosten
(*pl*)

market share Marktanteil, der (-e)

maturity (e.g. time to maturity) Fälligkeit,
die

member (of a company) Aktionär, der
(-e) (in AG), Gesellschafter, der (-) (in
GmbH), Anteilseigner, der (-) (in GmbH)

member of a group Konzernmitglied,
das (-er)

member of a group of undertakings
Konzernmitglied, das (-er)

memorandum (of a company) Satzung,
die (-en)

**memorandum and articles of
association** (= a company's own
rules) Satzung, die (-en)

merchandise [US] Ware, die (-n)/
Handelsware, die (-n)

merger Verschmelzung, die

middle exchange rate (on a daily basis)
Mittelkurs, der (-e)

mineral oil tax Mineralölsteuer, die

minority interest shareholder
konzernfremder Gesellschafter

minority interests* (= minority
shareholders' part in the consolidated
capital and reserves) Anteile im
Fremdbesitz/Anteile anderer
Gesellschafter

**minority interest in the profit or loss for
the current year** (= minority
shareholders' part in the consolidated
profit or loss) Anteile konzernfremder
am Jahresergebnis

mortgage Grundpfandrecht, das (-e)/
Pfandrecht an Grundstücken

movable tangible assets bewegliche
Sachanlagen (*pl*)

N

net (= after deductions) netto/saldiert

net book value (= original cost less
accumulated depreciation) Buchwert,
der (-e)

net income for the year [US]
Jahresüberschuß, der

**net income from investments in other
undertakings** (= comprises income
from participating interests,
associated and subsidiary
undertakings) Beteiligungsergebnis,
das

net interest (= interest receivable less
interest payable) Zinsergebnis, das

net off, to (against)
verrechnen/saldieren/aufrechnen (*sep*)
(gegeneinander)

net profit (= profit after all deductions for
expenditure, charges and tax)
Gewinn, der (-e)/Überschuß, der
(-üsse)

nominal capital (= limited liability capital at
nominal value in accounts)
gezeichnetes Kapital

nominal value (e.g. 50p shares have a
nominal value of 50p) Nominalwert,
der (-e)

notes to the financial statements
Anhang, der

O

obligation Verpflichtung, die (-en)/
Verbindlichkeit, die (-en)

occupational accident insurance
Berufsgenossenschaft, die (-en),
Berufsunfallversicherung, die (-en)

office fixtures and fittings
Geschäftsausstattung, die (-en)

office supplies Bürobedarf, der

old age social security system
Altersversorgung, die

operating charges
Betriebsaufwendungen (*pl*)

operating income betriebliche
Erträge/Betriebserlöse (*pl*)

operating profit or loss Ergebnis der
betrieblichen Tätigkeit/Ergebnis aus
Betriebstätigkeit

operating result Ergebnis der

betrieblichen Tätigkeit/Ergebnis aus Betriebstätigkeit

operating revenue [US] betriebliche Erträge/Betriebserlöse (*pl*)

operation Betrieb, der (-e), betrieblicher Prozeß

order (e.g. purchase order, customer/sales order) Bestellung, die (-en)

ordinary share Stammaktie, die (-n)

other current assets sonstige Vermögensgegenstände

other interest receivable and similar income* sonstige Zinsen und ähnliche Erträge

other operating charges* sonstige betriebliche Aufwendungen

other operating income* sonstige betriebliche Erträge

other operating revenue [US] sonstige betriebliche Erträge

other plant andere Anlagen

other provisions* sonstige Rückstellungen

other revenue reserves andere Gewinnrücklagen

other social costs Aufwendungen für Unterstützung

other taxes sonstige Steuern

output of goods and services for own purposes Eigenleistung, die (-en)

'outside funds' (= money raised from parties outside a company, e.g. banks) Fremdkapital, das

overdraft Verbindlichkeit gegenüber einem Kreditinstitut

overdraft facility Überziehungskredit, der (-e)

overhead costs Gemeinkosten (*pl*)

overheads Gemeinkosten (*pl*)

'own funds' (= money raised from within a company, e.g. shareholders) Eigenkapital, das

own shares* (the company itself – as a separate legal entity – purchased its own shares) eigene Anteile (in GmbH), eigene Aktien (in AG)

own work capitalised* (= internally produced and capitalised assets) aktivierte Eigenleistungen

owner Inhaber, der (-)

P

parent company Muttergesellschaft, die (-en)

parent undertaking Muttergesellschaft, die (-en)

participate, to (e.g. in a company) beteiligt sein

participating interest (= holding/stake/interest in a company) Beteiligung, die (-en)/Anteil, der (-e)

participation [US] (= holding/stake/interest in a company) Beteiligung, die (-en)/Anteil, der (-e)

par value (e.g. 50p shares have a par value of 50p) Nominalwert, der (-e)

patent Patent, das (-e)

pay Lohn, der (-öhne)

payable to affiliated enterprises [US] Verbindlichkeiten gegenüber verbundenen Unternehmen

payable to enterprises in which participations are held [US] Verbindlichkeiten gegenüber Unternehmen, mit denen ein Beteiligungsverhältnis besteht

payments on account (= advance payments made to suppliers of stocks or assets) geleistete Anzahlungen

payments received on account of customer orders erhaltene Anzahlungen auf Bestellungen

payroll costs Personalaufwand, der/Personalkosten (*pl*)

pending business/project/transactions (= both parties to a contract have not yet met their respective obligations, no goods/services or money have as yet been transferred) schwebende Geschäfte

pension costs Aufwendungen für Altersversorgung

period of use Nutzungsdauer, die

permit Lizenz, die (-en)

personnel costs Personalaufwand, der/Personalkosten (*pl*)

personnel costs additional to employee remuneration (= employer's contributions and voluntary social costs, e.g. training courses) Personalnebenkosten (*pl*)

petty cash Kassenbestand, der
(-ände)/Geldbestände (*pl*)

plant Anlage, die (-n)

plant and machinery* (e.g. technical
equipment, factory machines, tools)
technische Anlagen

plant building in progress Anlagenbau,
der

post, to (to an account) buchen

postage Porto

postal giro deposit Postgiroguthaben,
das (-)

post-balance sheet events Vorgänge
von besonderer Bedeutung seit Ende
des Geschäftsjahres

preference share Vorzugsaktie, die
(-n)/Vorrechtsaktie, die (-en)/
Prioritätsaktie, die (-en)

preferred stock [US] Vorzugsaktie, die
(-n)/Vorrechtsaktie, die (-en)/
Prioritätsaktie, die (-en)

premium (on interest-bearing
investments) Agio, das/Aufgeld, das

prepaid expenses [US] (= advance
payments to suppliers of stocks or
assets) geleistete Anzahlungen

prepaid tax Steuerabgrenzungsposten,
der (-) (*aktiv*)

prepare, to (annual report) aufstellen
(*sep*)

prepayment (= payment made in
advance)
Rechnungsabgrenzungsposten, der (-)
(*aktiv*), Vorauszahlung, die (-en)

**probable losses from incomplete
contracts** drohende Verluste aus
schwebenden Geschäften

proceeds Ertrag, der (-äge)/Erlös der (-e)

production material Fertigungsmaterial,
das (-ien)

professional association
Berufsvertretung, die (-en)

professional body Berufsvertretung, die
(-en)

profit Gewinn, der (-e)

profit and loss account
Erfolgsrechnung, die (-en)/Gewinn-
und Verlustrechnung, die (-en)

profit attributable to minority interests
(i.e. minority shareholders)
konzernfremden Gesellschaftern
zustehender Gewinn

profit brought forward (= previous years'
profits accumulated) Gewinnvortrag,
der (-äge)

profit for the financial year (= annual net
profit) Jahresüberschuß, der

profit on the sale of fixed assets
Gewinne aus dem Verkauf von
Sachanlagen

profit on the sale of shares Gewinne
aus dem Verkauf von Beteiligungen

profit or loss on ordinary activities
Ergebnis der gewöhnlichen
Geschäftstätigkeit

profit or loss for the year
Jahresergebnis, das

profit transfer Gewinnübernahme, die
(-n)

profit transfer contract
Gewinnabführvertrag, der (-äge)

provision (= estimate of expected future
expense or of anticipated future loss,
exact amount and timing not yet known;
long-term or short-term item)
Rückstellung, die (-en)

provision for deferred taxation
Rückstellung für latente Steuern

provision for insurances
versicherungstechnische Rückstellung

provisions for liabilities and charges* (=
estimates of expected future charges
and anticipated future losses, exact
amount and timing not yet known;
long-term and short-term items)
Rückstellungen (*pl*)

provisions for litigation costs
Prozeßrückstellungen (*pl*)

**provisions for pensions and similar
obligations** Rückstellungen für
Pensionen und ähnliche
Verpflichtungen

purchase contract Einkaufskontrakt, der
(-e)

purchase costs Anschaffungskosten
(*pl*)

purchase prices Anschaffungskosten
(*pl*)

purchased goods bezogene Waren

purchased merchandise [US] bezogene
Waren

purchased services bezogene
Leistungen

R

raise, to (e.g. capital) aufnehmen (*sep*)
rate 1. Satz, der (-ätze), 2. Kurs, der (-e), 3. Rate, die (-n)
rate of contribution Beitragssatz, der (-ätze)
rate of exchange Kurs, der (-e)
rationalisation measure Rationalisierungsmaßnahme, die (-n)
raw material Rohstoff, der (-e)
real estate (= land which may include buildings) Grundbesitz, der
real property (= land which may include buildings) Grundbesitz, der
rebate Rabatt, der (-e)
receivable [US] 1. Forderung, die (-en), 2. Kunde, der (-n)
receivables from affiliated enterprises [US] Forderungen gegen verbundene Unternehmen
receivables from enterprises in which participations are held [US] Forderungen gegen Unternehmen, mit denen ein Beteiligungsverhältnis besteht
reclassify, to (e.g. assets) umbuchen
redemption (= paying back/off) Tilgung, die (-en)/Rückzahlung, die (-en)
reducing-balance depreciation degressive Abschreibung
reduction in value Wertminderung, die (-en)
refund Erstattung, die (-en)
remaining period (e.g. for loan repayments) Restlaufzeit, die (-en)
rent Miete, die (-en)
rent prepayment Mietvorauszahlung, die (-en)
rent obligations Mietverpflichtungen (*pl*)
rental income Mieteinnahmen (*pl*)
rented property Mietobjekt, das (-e)
repair and maintenance Instandhaltung, die
repayment (paying back/off e.g. a loan) Tilgung, die (-en), Rückzahlung, die (-en)
replacement costs Wiederbeschaffungskosten (*pl*)
reproduction costs Wiederherstellungskosten (*pl*)
residual time to maturity (= remaining period up to date of payment) Restlaufzeit, die (-en)

retained profits (= profits not distributed to shareholders) nicht ausgeschüttete Gewinne / thesaurierte Gewinne
retirement Pensionierung, die (-en)
retirement benefit Pension, die (-en)
retirement pension Pension, die (-en)
research and development Forschung und Entwicklung
reserve (= set aside fund) Rücklage, die (-n)
reserve for own shares* Rücklage für eigene Anteile
reserve provided for by the articles of association* satzungsmäßige Rücklage
result Ergebnis, das (-se)
result (= net total of profit and loss transfers) **from interests in associated undertakings** Ergebnis aus assoziierten Unternehmen
revenue Erlös, der (-e), Einnahmen (*pl*)
revenue reserve (= accumulated retained profits) Gewinnrücklage, die (-n)
reversal of provisions (= previously expected expenses did not occur and are therefore cancelled) Auflösung von Rückstellungen
risk Risiko, das (-ken)
risks with contractual commitments/pending projects Risiken aus schwebenden Geschäften
road tax Kraftfahrzeugsteuer, die

S

salary Gehalt, das (-älter)
sale Verkauf, der (-äufe)
sales Umsätze (*pl*)
sales commission Verkaufsprovision, die (-en)
sales contract Verkaufskontrakt, der (-e)
sales revenue(s) (= sales in money terms) Umsatz, der, Umsatzerlöse (*pl*)
sales volume (= sales in quantity terms) Umsatz, der
scheduled (depreciation) planmäßig
secondary business activity Nebengeschäft, das (-e)
sector of industry Branche, die (-n)
securities Wertpapiere (*pl*)
security Sicherheit, die (-en)

security [US] (e.g. stocks and shares, loan-notes, bonds, etc.) Wertpapier, das (-e)

selling rate (of currencies) Briefkurs, der

semi-finished halbfertig

semi-finished goods halbfertige Erzeugnisse

service Dienstleistung, die (-en)/ Leistung, die (-en)

services provided but not invoiced nicht abgerechnete Leistungen

set off (against), to (= to net off) verrechnen

settle, to (e.g. an account) abrechnen

setting-up of provisions Bildung von Rückstellungen

share Aktie, die (-n) (in AG), Anteil, der (-e) (in GmbH), Geschäftsanteil, der (-e) (in GmbH)

share capital (= all types of shares in a company) Grundkapital, das (in AG), Stammkapital, das (in GmbH)

share capital and reserves (=shareholders' fund) Eigenkapital, das

shareholding Geschäftsanteil, der (-e)/ Aktienbestand, der (-ände)

shareholder Aktionär, der (-e) (in AG), Gesellschafter, der (-) (in GmbH), Anteilseigner, der (-) (in GmbH)

shareholders' equity [US] (= capital and reserves) Eigenkapital, das

shareholders' fund (= capital and reserves) Eigenkapital, das

share premium (= difference between the nominal value of a share and its market value, e.g. 10p shares traded at £2.10 have a nominal value of 10p and a share premium of £2) Agio, das

share premium account (= accumulated share premiums) Kapitalrücklage, die (-n)

shares in affiliated enterprises [US] Anteile an verbundenen Unternehmen

shares in associated enterprises [US] Anteile an assoziierten Unternehmen

shares in associated undertakings Anteile an assoziierten Unternehmen

shares in group undertakings Anteile an verbundenen Unternehmen

sign, to (the auditor) testieren

social fund for employees (to compensate employees affected by changes in business operations, e.g. plant closure or change in plant location) Sozialplan, der (-äne)

social security soziale Sicherheit

social security costs* Sozialkosten (pl)/soziale Aufwendungen/soziale Abgaben

sound commercial judgement vernünftige kaufmännische Beurteilung

source of funds Mittelherkunft, die

source of income Einkommensquelle, die (-n)

special depreciation Sonderabschreibung, die (-)

special position/post/item Sonderposten, der (-)

special tax-allowable reserve (contains retained profits as well as the respective tax payable) Sonderposten mit Rücklageanteil

staff costs Personalaufwand, der/ Personalkosten (pl)

staff costs additional to employee remuneration (= employer's contributions and voluntary social costs, e.g. training courses) Personalnebenkosten (pl)

staff training Personalausbildung, die (-en)

start-up of a business Ingangsetzung, die

statement of earnings [US] Erfolgsrechnung, die (-en)/Gewinn- und Verlustrechnung, die (-en)

stationery Bürobedarf, der

statutory reserve [US] satzungsmäßige Rücklage

stock changes (= change in stocks of finished goods and in work-in-progress) Bestandsveränderungen (pl)

stock exchange Börse, die (-n)

stockholder [US] Aktionär, der (-e) (in AG), Gesellschafter, der (-) (in GmbH), Anteilseigner, der (-) (in GmbH)

stockholding [US] Geschäftsanteil, der (-e)/Aktienbestand, der (-ände)

stocks* Vorräte (pl)/Bestand, der/ Bestände (pl)

stocktaking Bestandsaufnahme, die (-n)

straight-line depreciation lineare Abschreibung

subscribed capital [US] (= capital with limited liability) gezeichnetes Kapital

subsidiary Tochtergesellschaft, die (-en)
subsidiary company Tochtergesellschaft, die (-en)
subsidiary undertaking verbundenes Unternehmen
subsidy Zuschuß, der (-üsse)
subtract, to absetzen (*sep*)
sundry expenses übrige Aufwendungen
sundry operating charges übrige betriebliche Aufwendungen
sundry operating income übrige betriebliche Erträge
sundry overheads sonstige Gemeinkosten
sundry sales andere Erlöse
supplier Lieferant, der (-en)/Lieferer, der (-)
supplies [US] (e.g. single-use factory materials, small tools) Hilfs- und Betriebsstoffe (*pl*)
supply Lieferung, die (-en)
surplus Überschuß, der (-üsse)

T

take out, to (e.g. a loan) aufnehmen (*sep*)
tangible fixed asset Anlagegut, das (-üter)/Sachanlage, die (-n)
tangible fixed assets Sachanlagen (*pl*)
tax Steuer, die (-n)
taxation (= imposition of taxes) Besteuerung, die (-en)
'tax' balance sheet Steuerbilanz, die (-en)
tax credit Steuergutschrift, die (-en)
tax-free reserves (profits transferred Into these reserves are temporarily not taxed) steuerfreie Rücklagen
tax on assets Vermögensteuer, die
tax on assets levied by local government (= similar to UK council taxes) Gewerbekapitalsteuer, die
tax on bills of exchange Wechselsteuer, die
tax on insurances Versicherungsteuer, die
tax on investment income (= tax on dividends, interest, etc.) Kapitalertragsteuer, die
tax on land levied by local government (= similar to UK council taxes) Grundsteuer, die
tax law Steuerrecht, das, Steuergesetz, das

tax on profits levied by local government (= similar to UK council taxes) Gewerbeertragsteuer, die
tax provision Steuerrückstellung, die (-en)
tax refund Erstattung, die (-en)
tax refunds for previous years Erstattungen für Vorjahre
taxes on income [US] Steuern vom Einkommen und vom Ertrag/Ertragsteuer
taxes on profit Steuern vom Einkommen und vom Ertrag/Ertragsteuer
telephone costs Telefonkosten (*pl*)
term Laufzeit, die (-en)
trade 1. Handel, der, 2. Gewerbe, das (-), 3. Branche, die (-n)
trade credit Lieferantenkredit, der (-e)
trade creditors* Verbindlichkeiten aus Lieferungen und Leistungen (von Lieferanten)
trade debtors* Forderungen aus Lieferungen und Leistungen (an Kunden)
trade mark Warenzeichen, das (-)
trade payables [US] Verbindlichkeiten aus Lieferungen und Leistungen (von Lieferanten)
trade receivables [US] Forderungen aus Lieferungen und Leistungen (an Kunden)
trading business Handelsfirma, die (-en)
transfer Umbuchung, die (-en)/Einstellung, die (-en)
transfer from, to (e.g. transfer from a reserve) umbuchen/entnehmen
transfer from revenue reserves Entnahmen aus Gewinnrücklagen
transfer to, to (e.g. transfer to a reserve) umbuchen/einstellen
transfer to revenue reserves Einstellung in Gewinnrücklagen
transfer to special tax-allowable reserve Einstellung in Sonderposten mit Rücklageanteil
translate, to (e.g. currencies) umrechnen
travel expenses Reisekosten (*pl*)/Reiseaufwendungen (*pl*)
turnover* Umsatzerlöse (*pl*)
turnover before tax Bruttoergebnis vom Umsatz

U

uncollectible receivables [US] uneinbringliche Forderungen/Forderungsausfälle

uncompleted services unfertige Leistungen

undertaking (= any form of business e.g. company, partnership, unincorporated association) Unternehmen, das (-)

underwriting business Versicherungsgeschäft, das (-e)

unemployment insurance Arbeitslosenversicherung, die

unfinished goods unfertige Erzeugnisse

upward trend Aufwärtsentwicklung, die

V

vacation pay [US] Urlaubsgehalt, das (-älter)/Urlaubsentgelt, das (-e)

valuation Wertansatz, der (-ätze)

value-added tax Umsatzsteuer, die

voluntary expenditure for staff freiwillige soziale Aufwendungen

voting right Stimmrecht, das (-e)

W

wages Lohn, der (-öhne)

wages and salaries Löhne und Gehälter

wages in manufacture Fertigungslohn, der (-öhne)

weakness in the economy Konjunkturschwäche, die

wind up, to (e.g. a company) liquidieren

within a group konzernintern

within the framework of social security im Rahmen der sozialen Sicherheit

work-in-process [US] halbfertige Erzeugnisse, unfertige Erzeugnisse, unfertige Leistungen

work-in-progress* halbfertige Erzeugnisse, unfertige Erzeugnisse, unfertige Leistungen

world economy Weltkonjunktur, die

world sales Weltumsatz, der (-ätze)

world trade Welthandel, der

world turnover Weltumsatz, der (-ätze)

write off, to (e.g. bad debts) ausbuchen

write-down of financial assets and short-term investments [US] Abschreibungen auf Finanzanlagen und auf Wertpapiere des Umlaufvermögens

writing back of provisions (= previously expected expenses did not occur and are therefore cancelled) Auflösung von Rückstellungen

Appendix

Der Aufbau einer deutschen Bilanz

AKTIVA	PASSIVA
A ANLAGEVERMÖGEN	A EIGENKAPITAL
I Immaterielle Vermögensgegenstände II Sachanlagen III Finanzanlagen	I Gezeichnetes Kapital II Kapitalrücklage III Gewinnrücklagen IV Gewinnvortrag/Verlustvortrag V Jahresüberschuß/Jahresehlbetrag
B UMLAUFVERMÖGEN	
I Vorräte II Forderungen und sonstige Vermögensgegenstände III Wertpapiere IV Flüssige Mittel	*SONDERPOSTEN MIT RÜCKLAGEANTEIL* B RÜCKSTELLUNGEN
	C VERBINDLICHKEITEN
C RECHNUNGSABGRENZUNGS- POSTEN	D RECHNUNGSABGRENZUNGS- POSTEN

(Bezeichnungen der Überschriften gemäß HGB)

The structure of a German balance sheet

ASSETS	CAPITAL AND LIABILITIES
A FIXED ASSETS*	A CAPITAL AND RESERVES*
I Intangible assets*	I Nominal capital
II Tangible assets*	II Capital reserve
III Investments*	III Revenue reserves
	IV Profit and loss account brought forward
	V Profit or loss for the year
B CURRENT ASSETS*	
I Stocks*	*SPECIAL TAX-ALLOWABLE RESERVE*
II Debtors and other current assets	
III Investments*	B PROVISIONS FOR LIABILITIES AND CHARGES*
IV Cash at bank and in hand*	
	C CREDITORS
C PREPAYMENTS AND ACCRUED INCOME*	D ACCRUALS AND DEFERRED INCOME*

(Numbering and lettering according to HGB)